WITHDRAWN

The Themes of
HENRY JAMES

A System of Observation through the Visual Arts

BY EDWIN T. BOWDEN

Instructor in English, Yale University

Archon Books   1969

© Copyright 1956 by Yale University Press
Reprinted 1969 with permission of Yale University Press
in an unaltered and unabridged edition

[*Yale Studies in English, Vol. 132*]

SBN: 208 00723 7
Library of Congress Catalog Card Number: 69-18270
Printed in the United States of America

Therefore it is that experience has to organise, for convenience and cheer, some system of observation—for fear, in the admirable immensity, of losing its way. We see it as pausing from time to time to consult its notes, to measure, for guidance, as many aspects and distances as possible, as many steps taken and obstacles mastered and fruits gathered and beauties enjoyed. Everything counts, nothing is superfluous in such a survey; the explorer's note-book strikes me here as endlessly receptive. This accordingly is what I mean by the contributive value— or put it simply as, to one's own sense, the beguiling charm—of the *accessory* facts in a given artistic case.

Preface to *Roderick Hudson*

A Preliminary Note

IN the last few decades, the novels of Henry James have received increasingly the critical attention which they deserve. Before more is offered, a few words of explanation seem called for. In a doctoral dissertation at Yale University, the origin of this book, written under the guidance and encouragement of Stanley T. Williams, I attempted to explain James' use of the visual arts in his novels. While exploring that more or less mechanical subject, I found that the arts offered a "system of observation," a method of interpretative approach to the novels, that was critically valid, and in particular offered a convenient means of grasping the central themes. It is common knowledge that James' novels, particularly the later ones, are difficult reading. Despite the sizable amount of criticism available, however, there is little, with a few notable exceptions, which will help the average reader—a misnomer, for no reader of James can be average—with his struggle for understanding. To my delight, the approach to the novels through the visual arts, coupled with a reasonable amount of straightforward comment, offered just the sort of interpretation needed. At the same time it offered the scholar, the devotee, and the more advanced student an interpretation which often differed, I believe correctly so, from the commonly accepted. This book is the result.

Others before me, of course, have touched on the subject and the method. F. O. Matthiessen in the criticism culminating in *Henry James: The Major Phase* has done the most notable work, although several articles by others deserve praise, particularly Adeline R. Tintner's "The Spoils of Henry James," *PMLA, 61* (March, 1946), 239–51, and Miriam Allott's "Symbol and Image in the Later Work of Henry James," *Essays in Criticism, 3* (July, 1953), 321–36. Since the subject is so fruitful, it is inevitable that many critics have taken up smaller points here and there. As a general rule I have made no attempt to take issue with other critics or to use their conclusions to strengthen my own. My primary purpose has been to present a valid reading of the novels, concentrating on their central themes, and to establish a means of attaining such a reading; scholarly apparatus has been kept to a minimum, and with one or two exceptions I have restricted my discussion to the texts themselves.

As a background to such concentration, however, and as a matter of interest in itself, I have devoted the first chapter to a biographical account of Henry James' personal relationship with the visual arts.

Those familiar with James' dedication to art in all its forms, whether visual or literary, will immediately recognize the relevance of this chapter to his thought and to his work as a whole. But the relevance is an even greater one than might at first appear, for the critical value of the visual arts in the novels grows directly from, and in fact is dependent upon, the values and the meaning which James himself found in the arts. The novels in sum do make those values apparent, and offer without need for outside aid the necessary understanding of the meaning of the arts in the individual novel. But some preliminary biographical knowledge is an aid to more immediate understanding, as well as perhaps a more complete understanding. Here the value of biographical knowledge to literary criticism is a valid one.

The great collection of James' letters at Harvard University has been of inestimable value in the biographical research, and I should like to extend my thanks to William A. Jackson of the Houghton Library. In its original version, the first chapter was completed before the appearance of Leon Edel's *Henry James: The Untried Years, 1843–1870,* Philadelphia and New York, 1953, but his work has offered useful corroboration. The Yale University Library has also been of particular aid in the problem of texts. The great majority of James' novels exist in at least two and sometimes three or more differing texts. The collected New York Edition of 1907–09 presents the most complete revision, but in some instances a novel underwent several revisions before that final one. At first glance the use of the latest revised text for discussion would seem the natural choice, particularly since in the process of revision the imagery was greatly amplified and made more striking. This amplification would undoubtedly strengthen my discussion of the earlier novels. On the other hand, the use of the latest text of those novels appearing in the New York Edition would blur and even distort the view of the chronological development of James' powers and achievements, for it would present not the James of the time of composition but that James tempered and at times even confused by the James of the early nineteen-hundreds. The texts used here are the original ones, the first American edition in book form for the sake of convenience and uniformity. The interpretation and the method of reaching it is, of course, equally valid for the revised texts, and the interested reader will find there, particularly in James' youthful novels, even more material with which to work and even stronger proof of the critical conclusions.

For greater ease in reading, ellipsis dots have not been used at the beginning or end of quotations to indicate an incomplete sentence. In the notes, reference to any work of James is to the first American edition, defined by LeRoy Phillips' *A Bibliography of the Writings of*

A PRELIMINARY NOTE xi

Henry James, new ed. New York, Coward: McCann, 1930. The first reference to each work is complete; subsequently shorter forms are used. For the sake of brevity, James' name is not given for his own works; where the name of no author appears, the author is James. In references to letters, the abbreviation *Letters* is used for *The Letters of Henry James,* ed. Percy Lubbock (2 vols. New York, Charles Scribner's Sons, 1920), and the abbreviation HL for the Houghton Library, Harvard University.

I wish to express my appreciation to the Harvard University Library, to the Yale University Library, and to Paul R. Reynolds and Son, 599 Fifth Avenue, New York, for permission to quote from unpublished letters of Henry James. For permission to make quotations from copyrighted material I am also indebted to Charles Scribner's Sons, Harper & Brothers, Houghton Mifflin Co., the Macmillan Co., Oxford University Press, and William Sloane Associates. My particular and most personal gratitude goes to those friends and associates who have offered encouragement and needed criticism: to the late Stanley T. Williams, a friend and advisor from the beginning, to the members of the Yale English Department who read the manuscript in its several versions, and to Benjamin C. Nangle, whose editorial aid has been great. To my wife, Ann Bowden, no thanks are possible; without her it would have been too long and lonely a way.

December 15, 1955 EDWIN T. BOWDEN

Contents

A Preliminary Note		ix
1.	The Man and the Arts	1
	James' lifelong interest in the arts. The observer, the traveler, the professional critic. His personal preferences and esthetic principles. His analogy of the novel and the arts.	
2.	The European-American Theme: Europe	23
	The value of the arts as a system of observation. The definition of the theme. Initial definition in *Roderick Hudson*. *The American* as fulfillment of the theme.	
3.	The European-American Theme: America	37
	James tiring of European theme: *Confidence, The Reverberator*. The definition of the American theme in *Washington Square* and *The Bostonians*. *The Europeans* as fulfillment of the theme.	
4.	The Theme of Moral Decision	53
	The moral-esthetic relationship as dramatization and definition. Transition, introduction, and initial fulfillment in *The Portrait of a Lady*. Variations on the theme: *The Princess Casamassima, The Tragic Muse*. *The Spoils of Poynton* as fulfillment of the theme.	
5.	The Experiments and the Conjunction of Themes	78
	Experiments in the art of the novel: dramatic presentation in *The Other House, The Awkward Age, The Outcry;* the reflector in *What Maisie Knew;* the prying observer in *The Sacred Fount*. *The Wings of the Dove* as fulfillment of the conjunction of themes.	
6.	The Final Synthesis of Themes	97
	The Ambassadors and *The Golden Bowl* as continued fulfillment of the final synthesis of themes. A backward glance in summary and conclusion: the "line of continuity" in the man and the novels.	
Index		117

I

The Man and the Arts

IN *A Small Boy and Others* Henry James describes the most vivid nightmare of his life, a dream in which he pursued a dimly seen figure down a long glorious hall suddenly revealed as the Galerie d'Apollon of the Louvre, the gallery in which he had found such fascination as a boy. The dream deserves mention in James' history, for it points to the predominant place held in his mind, conscious and subconscious, youthful and mature, by the art gallery and the visual arts which it represented. He himself after relating the dream calls his perceptions of the Louvre "educative, formative, fertilising, in a degree which no other 'intellectual experience' our youth was to know could pretend, as a comprehensive, conducive thing, to rival." [1] The volumes of autobiographical reminiscence, *A Small Boy and Others* (1913), *Notes of a Son and Brother* (1914), and the unfinished *The Middle Years* (1917), illustrate the comment at length, for they are full of references to the arts, memories of his own and his brother's painting, intimations of the importance of the arts to his intellectual growth. Since in the novels of his maturity the visual arts are equally present, and there have a high critical value, the history of the young James' relationship with the arts deserves attention as one element of the seminal development of his powers as a novelist, or as he would have preferred, his powers as an artist.

Most important to him for the relationship, important as a foundation for his own knowledge and for his later continued interest, was his own early dabbling in art. As a small boy he enjoyed drawing, and as a man told with some amusement his early attempts at play writing, in which every fourth page was an illustration, and the drawing of these illustrations was more fun than the writing. The effect of such play on his mature pictorial vision in the novel is an interesting speculation. Later, the boy's first years in Europe were spent happily painting with his brother William: "I see again that we but endlessly walked and endlessly daubed, and that our walks, with an obsession of their own, constantly abetted our daubing." [2] But Henry's great opportunity came when the family returned from Europe in 1860 to place William, who had for the moment decided on a career in art, under

---

1. *A Small Boy and Others* (New York, Charles Scribner's Sons, 1913), p. 349.
2. Ibid., p. 308.

the tutelage of the distinguished American artist William Morris Hunt.

There in Newport Henry happily accompanied his brother William to the studio. No matter with how little success he worked, he later felt the time had been of importance to his development:

> Frankly, intensely—that was the great thing—these were hours of Art, art definitely named, looking me full in the face and accepting my stare in return—no longer a tacit implication or a shy subterfuge, but a flagrant unattenuated aim. I had somehow come into the temple by the back door, the *porte d'honneur* opened on another side, and I could never have believed much at best in the length of my stay; but I was there, day by day, as much as anyone had ever been, and with a sense of what it "meant" to be there . . . so that the situation to this extent really hummed with promise.[3]

As his interest gradually turned from the visual arts to the literary, aided and encouraged by John La Farge, the noted painter then visiting the family and also studying under Hunt, Henry remained in the atmosphere of the arts, and felt the close relation between his own form of art and that about him: "If somewhat later on I could still so fondly hang about in that air of production . . . it was altogether in the form of mere helpless admirer and inhaler, led captive in part by the dawning perception that the arts were after all essentially one and that even with canvas and brush whisked out of my grasp I still needn't feel disinherited."[4] The early period of boyish drawing and more or less formal study had given him a basis of knowledge and interest that was to last all his life, and to influence profoundly the theory and practice of his novels.

James was to know many artists in his life, a list would fill several pages, but William Hunt remained, from memories of youth, "in every accent and motion, the living and communicating Artist."[5] Whatever he taught the boy about art, and however he improved his taste, Hunt's greatest contribution to James' education was in the "truly fertilising action"[6] of the example he set, "a manner and range of gesture and broken form of discourse that was like a restless reference to a palette and that seemed to take for granted, all about, canvases and models and charming, amusing things, the 'tremendously interesting' in the seen bit or caught moment, and the general unsayability, in comparison, of anything else."[7] John La Farge, present at the same time, and

---

3. *Notes of a Son and Brother* (New York, Charles Scribner's Sons, 1914), p. 81.
4. Ibid., p. 97.
5. Ibid., p. 83.
6. Ibid., p. 79.
7. Ibid., pp. 83-4.

a lifelong friend, also emphasized for the boy the importance of art and taste to the sensitive mind: "Our guest . . . began meanwhile to paint, under our eyes, with devotion, with exquisite perception, and above all as with the implication, a hundred times beneficent and fertilising, that if one didn't in these connections consistently take one's stand on supersubtlety of taste one was a helpless outsider and at the best the basest of vulgarians or flattest of frauds." [8] For Henry he represented the full life, Europe and art and literature, "an esthetic nature of wondrous homogeneity," [9] and it is fitting that it was La Farge who led him to the literature of France, and encouraged him in his early writing.

Henry James' early and serious interest in art was hardly unusual, for the interest was a family characteristic. In *Notes of a Son and Brother* he writes, "It was an odd enough circumstance, in respect to the attested blood in our veins, that no less than three of our father's children, with two of his grandsons to add to these, and with a collateral addendum representing seven, in all, of our grandfather's, William James's, descendants in three generations, should have found the artistic career in general and the painter's trade in particular irresistibly solicit them." [1] Surrounded as he was by artists in the family, his interest could only be kept alive. "As I catch W. J.'s image, from far back, at its most characteristic, he sits drawing and drawing, always drawing . . . ; and not as with a plodding patience, which I think would less have affected me, but easily, freely and, as who should say, infallibly: always at the stage of finishing off, his head dropped from side to side and his tongue rubbing his lower lip." [2] The brilliantly arrested image of William might well stand as one of the symbols of Henry James' youth.

Beyond his boyhood at home, however, James still found artists in the family. He admired his younger brother Bob, a man seriously concerned with painting, particularly during the eighties, and often praised his artistic ability: "He had an admirable hand and eye, and I have known no other such capacity for absorbing or storing up the minutest truths and shades of landscape fact and giving them out afterward, in separation from the scene, with full assurance and felicity." [3] Later in his life Henry took a particular interest in the painting of Bill James, Jr., and in that of "my brave little cousin Bay Emmet (the paintress)." [4] Several times he was able to have Bill with him at Lamb House and always gave genuine attention to his painting. After the

8. Ibid., p. 94.
9. Ibid., p. 91.
1. Ibid., p. 45.
2. *Small Boy*, p. 207.
3. *Son and Brother*, p. 38.
4. To Gaillard T. Lapsley, June 22, 1902, in *Letters, I*, 392.

summer of 1908 with Bill, he could even write with renewed interest to Bay Emmet, "I am infinitely and yearningly interested . . . in every invisible stroke of your brush, over which I ache for baffled curiosity or wonderment." [5] One can hardly spend a summer with an enthusiastic young painter without finding the subject of painting a matter of immediate and continued concern.

If James' relations with the artists in his own family and with William Hunt and John La Farge illustrate the effect of the artist on his education, his relations with John Singer Sargent might stand for his friendship with scores of other artists, and illustrate both his continued interest in the arts and even, indirectly, his contribution to the visual arts. In a number of letters James mentions seeing Sargent or dining with him, and he usually takes the opportunity of praising him: "The only Franco-American product of importance here strikes me as young John Sargent the painter, who has high talent, a charming nature, artistic & personal, & is civilized to his finger-tips." [6] Late in his life, as a gift and a tribute from his friends, James even sat for a portrait by the artist, famous by that time, and was well pleased with the result: "It is now finished, . . . and is nothing less evidently, than a very fine thing indeed, Sargent at his very best and poor H. J. not at his worst; in short a living breathing likeness and a masterpiece of painting." [7]

Some idea of James' friendship with Sargent, as well as of his acquaintance with the London art world in general, may be gained from an unpublished letter of 1884 describing several days which James spent in showing Sargent about the city. He tells of taking the almost unknown painter to an exhibit of Sir Joshua Reynolds, to the National Gallery, and to the theater, and adds, with a poignant show of envy,

> I took him to 10 artists' studios, to see the pictures just going to the exhibitions; & at 8 o'clock entertained him at dinner at the Reform Club, where I had six men to meet him. Burne Jones was one of these—& was in very good form, as they say here. Sargent is the nicest creature possible. . . . One of the studios we went to yesterday was Millais's—another was Leighton's; & I was impressed, as usual, with the gorgeous effect of worldly prosperity & success that both of these gentlemen present.[8]

A more interesting aspect of the friendship, however, is seen in another unpublished letter of 1884:

> We are in the midst of the explosion of exhibitions; most of which are plentifully stocked with "rot." The Academy is "filthy." The

---

5. To Miss Ellen Emmet, Nov. 2, 1908, in *Letters, 2*, 108.
6. Copy of letter to Miss Grace Norton, Feb. 23, 1884, in HL.
7. To Miss Rhoda Broughton, June 25, 1913, in *Letters, 2*, 318.
8. Copy of letter to Miss Grace Norton, Mar. 29, 1884, in HL.

Grosvenor Gallery is better only in possessing a beautiful Burne-Jones. . . . A young friend of mine of whom I am very fond, & whose talent I think rare, (John Sargent) has sent over from Paris, through my mediation, a portrait which is universally gibed and jeered at—so that it is almost a personal discomfiture to me. He has a better—much better thing at the Academy—a big portrait of a pretty American woman (Mrs. White . . .) which *I* think far away, in style, tone, etc., the 1st portrait there & the only thing which touches a woman (with the brush) as a woman should be touched. But very few other people see that here (though Sargent has such a reputation in Paris,) & I am left to the consolations of my personal enthusiasm.[9]

James, then, could and did influence the London exhibitions, and could extend an active helping hand to the young artist for whom he felt a personal enthusiasm.

However the artists of his acquaintance may have served to stimulate his interest in the arts, it is James' direct acquaintance with and response to the arts themselves that provide the more important element of the relationship. His own early attempts at painting gave him an understanding and appreciation not to be gained from mere observation, but observation played an important part in his early life. Before the time of interest in the formal arts, perhaps even before any serious attempts of his own to draw, James was fascinated by illustrations in books. Supreme, as might be expected, were those of Phiz and Cruikshank for Dickens, although he mentions several others, particularly the steel engravings in a set of Pierre de Béranger, "to the strange imagery of which I so wonderingly responded that all other art of illustration, ever since, has been for me comparatively weak and cold."[1] Such illustrations so helped to form his youthful imagination that after prolonged acquaintance with one set devoted to the heroines of Shakespeare, "it was for long afterwards a shock . . . at the theatre not to see just those bright images, with their peculiar toggeries, come on."[2]

Illustration is perhaps a minor form of art—although James did not think so when he praised it in *Picture and Text*—but it is enough to foster an active interest in the major forms. And even as a young boy, before the European jaunts of 1855–60, James was finding delight in the formal art available to his fascinated gaze. The interest seemed natural enough to him: "My small 'interest in art,' that is my bent for gaping at illustrations and exhibitions, was absorbing and genuine. There were elements in the case that made it natural: the picture, the

---

9. Copy of letter to Miss Grace Norton, May 6 [1884], in HL.
1. *Small Boy*, p. 19.
2. Ibid., p. 96.

representative design, directly and strongly appealed to me, and was to appeal all my days, and I was only slow to recognise the *kind,* in this order, that appealed most." [3] For the moment the interest was served by the exhibitions in New York. The pictures, examples of the Düsseldorf school for the most part, were hardly the best, but they were impressive to a small boy: "Ineffable, unsurpassable those hours of initiation which the Broadway of the 'fifties had been, when all was said, so adequate to supply. If one wanted pictures there *were* pictures, as large, I seem to remember, as the side of a house, and of a bravery of colour and lustre of surface that I was never afterwards to see surpassed." [4]

A visit to an exhibition could be a matter of privileged pleasure, a special treat in which the large showy pictures seemed a satisfyingly breath-taking climax: "No impression . . . was half so momentous as that of the epoch-making masterpiece of Mr. Leutze, which showed us Washington crossing the Delaware in a wondrous flare of projected gaslight and with the effect of a revelation to my young sight of the capacity of accessories to 'stand out.' I live again in the thrill of that evening." [5] It was not necessary, however, to seek out pictures, for the James house was full of them. And even more entrancing to the young mind than pictures was the classic marble bust between the two back windows: "This image was known and admired among us as the Bacchante; she had come to us straight from an American studio in Rome, and I see my horizon flush again with the first faint dawn of conscious appreciation, or in other words of the critical spirit, while two or three of the more restrictive friends of the house find our marble lady very 'cold' for a Bacchante." [6] With interest aroused, as well as the first stirrings of the critical spirit, the young James was prepared to enjoy the art of Europe.

The two periods of European travel between 1855 and 1860 introduced him to great art, and began the formation of a taste that was to find its clearest statement in his period of professional art criticism in the seventies and eighties. The period in London, however, despite the greater availability of the arts, contributed to taste little more than the period in America. James haunted the Pantheon, given over for the most part to the huge pictures of B. R. Haydon. Of that time, while still vaguely wishing to be himself a painter, he says, "I blush to risk the . . . surmise that the grand manner, the heroic and the classic, in Haydon, came home to us more warmly and humanly than in the masters commended as 'old,' who, at the National Gallery, seemed to meet us so little half-way, . . . or suggest something that *we* could do, or

3. Ibid., p. 263.
4. Ibid., p. 265.
5. Ibid., pp. 266–7.
6. Ibid., p. 270.

could at least want to." [7] Then too, Henry and his brother William, like most boys, were unthinking admirers of the new and the modern. "If we adored daubing we preferred it *fresh*." [8] But the freshest and the most modern painting, in English public opinion, was the Pre-Raphaelite, and so quite naturally it found admirers in the boys: "The very word Pre-Raphaelite wore for us that intensity of meaning, not less than of mystery, that thrills us in its perfection but for one season." [9] Yet rising above the enthusiasms of youth, James felt even then an admiration for the English school of art which was to last all his life: "*They* were, by some deep-seated English mystery, the real unattainable, just as they were none the less the directly inspiring and the endlessly delightful." [1] At least the London period had that to offer to the maturing mind.

Paris, the next step in the esthetic education, had much more to offer. Even the streets, James later recalled, seemed to cry, " 'Art, art, art, don't you see? Learn, little gaping pilgrims, what *that* is!' " and the old houses to say, " 'Yes, small staring jeune homme, we are dignity and memory and measure, we are conscience and proportion and taste.' " [2] Under the guidance of William Hunt, Paris did indeed become a city of art, and Henry began haltingly to sense the compelling force of taste, a taste which he was later to admit seemed in that age so simple and so easy to grasp: "It was a comfortable time—when appreciation could go so straight, could rise, and rise higher, without critical contortions; when we could, I mean, be both so intelligent and so 'quiet.' " [3] Step by step he was led inexorably toward the Louvre. At first the great gallery was so overwhelming that it seemed to call for nothing more than bewildered appreciation. Yet appreciation was the beginning of discrimination, and the final step toward esthetic maturity. "In those beginnings I felt myself most happily cross that bridge over to Style constituted by the wondrous Galerie d'Apollon, drawn out for me as a long but assured initiation and seeming to form with its supreme coved ceiling and inordinately shining parquet a prodigious tube or tunnel through which I inhaled little by little, that is again and again, a general sense of *glory*." [4] With the Galerie d'Apollon, the scene of James' vivid nightmare, his primary education in the visual arts was complete.

The new maturity, particularly after the period in Newport with Hunt and La Farge, is found in a letter of 1867 to Thomas S. Perry: "Your talk about the Italian—especially the Venetian—pictures, went

7. Ibid., p. 314.
8. Ibid., p. 314.
9. Ibid., pp. 315–6.
1. Ibid., p. 315.
2. Ibid., p. 338.
3. Ibid., pp. 341–2.
4. Ibid., p. 346.

to my soul. Of all and of all things, those are what I want most to see." [5] Perhaps more obviously, it is found in the memory of his return to London in 1869, evoked so sensitively in the unfinished *The Middle Years*. There, for instance, he describes his visit to the National Gallery: "The great element was of course that I well-nigh incredibly stood again in the immediate presence of Titian and Rembrandt, of Rubens and Paul Veronese, and that the cup of sensation was thereby filled to overflowing." [6] James was no longer groping toward a sense of values and a personal taste. During that year he haunted the galleries of Europe with a sense of excitement conveyed in almost every letter, until he could write to his father, "I feel able to say with a certain amount of truth that I *know* the Uffizi & the Pitti. How much the wiser I am for my knowledge I hope one of these days to learn—if not to teach." [7] By 1870, at the age of twenty-seven, the last year covered by published reminiscences, James had established his sense of appreciation and was ready to enjoy it and to pass it on to others.

The further history of his interest is found for the most part in his travel sketches, collected in *Transatlantic Sketches* (1875), *Portraits of Places* (1883), *A Little Tour in France* (1885), *English Hours* (1905), *The American Scene* (1907), and *Italian Hours* (1909). Since his biographical study, *William Wetmore Story and His Friends* (1903), presents to some extent his personal view of the sculptor and his work, it too has autobiographical value. These sketches are particularly pertinent to the intensity of his mature interest in the arts, for in them James took every opportunity to discuss, or at least to describe, the works of art to be found in the regions through which he was passing. The sketches of Rome and Florence, for instance, are full of descriptions of architecture and painting and sculpture; so full, in fact, that they might almost pass as substitutes for the Baedeker. As James says in one, "I never see a leather curtain without lifting it; it is sure to cover a picture of some sort—good, bad, or indifferent." [8]

His personal letters after this initial period of travel, on the other hand, contain little direct description of individual works of art. Many of his correspondents were already familiar with the arts of Europe, and James had no intention of writing letters of polite description. Yet the letters do reveal two new interests which are not irrelevant to his esthetic history. In 1898 he moved into Lamb House at Rye in Sussex, and furnishing the new house was a challenge to taste and ingenuity. James,

---

5. To Thomas S. Perry, Aug. 15 [1867], in Virginia Harlow, *Thomas Sergeant Perry: a Biography; and Letters to Perry* . . . (Durham, N.C., Duke University Press, 1950), p. 281.
6. *The Middle Years*, ed. Percy Lubbock (New York, Charles Scribner's Sons, 1917), p. 50.
7. To father, Oct. 24 [1869?], in HL.
8. *Transatlantic Sketches* (Boston, James R. Osgood & Co., 1875), p. 119.

glorying in his bachelorhood, seems to have thoroughly enjoyed himself:

> In the meantime one must "pick up" a sufficient quantity of ancient mahogany-and-brass odds and ends—a task really the more amusing, here, where the resources are great, for having to be thriftily and cannily performed. The house is really quite charming enough in its particular character, and as to the stamp of its period, not to do violence to by rash modernities; and I am developing, under its influence and its inspiration, the most avid and gluttonous eye and most infernal watching patience, in respect of lurking "occasions" in not too-delusive Chippendale and Sheraton.[9]

Lamb House gave him a new personal interest in the visual arts, and another opportunity to try his own abilities. The other new interest, also indirectly creative, is seen in an unpublished letter to his literary agent, J. B. Pinker, in which he says of the forthcoming Uniform Edition, "The lettering strikes me as happy—a bigger or bolder would be out of keeping with the refined page. I take for granted the backs will be lettered congruously as well, even when the volume is slim. Such a cover and such a page will in short make, to my mind, very much the kind of pretty book we want."[1] The revival of an esthetic interest in printing, under the leadership of such men as William Morris, Emery Walker, and Charles Ricketts, had its effect on James, and his increasingly active interest in the physical appearance of his own books is reflected in his letters as well as in the books themselves.

However meaningful these new interests may be, they are minor in comparison with his immense response to the visual arts of Europe. In *Transatlantic Sketches* he wrote, "I am forever being reminded of the 'aesthetic luxury' . . . of living in Rome,"[2] and the remark might well represent his response to all of Europe. Pictures and palaces, statues and sketches, villas and remains all solicited his attention. The boy, ambitious to paint, was still present in the man, although the pen was substituted for the brush; and speaking of his joy in the "tone" of Rome he could even say, "I do not know that my immortal soul permanently suffers; it simply retires for a moment to give place to that of a hankering water-color sketcher."[3] In his early travels in Europe such a vision seemed particularly to add to the ubiquitous presence of the arts. Even the landscapes reminded him of painting: "Here and there in the distance, among blue undulations, some white village, some gray tower,

---

9. To Mrs. William James, Dec. 1, 1897, in *Letters, 1,* 266–7.
1. To J. B. Pinker, Nov. 12, 1914, in Yale University Library.
2. *Transatlantic Sketches,* p. 199.
3. Ibid., p. 129.

helped deliciously to make the scene the typical 'Italian landscape' of old-fashioned art." [4] All Europe was an enormous museum, and James gave it the same loving attention he had given the Louvre. The travel sketches show the attention, but the thrill of Europe for James is perhaps best shown in his glowing description in the biography of W. W. Story of the young sculptor's first descent on Italy. The personal quality of that description, the vicarious excitement felt by James, tells more clearly than any explicit statement the immense personal response which he felt to the great museum.

The response to the art of Europe was a response to Europe itself, for James felt that Europe and its arts were inseparable, each depending upon and explaining the other. In *Portraits of Places* he says of Venice: "Nowhere . . . do art and life seem so interfused and, as it were, so consanguineous. All the splendour of light and colour, all the Venetian air and the Venetian history, are on the walls and ceilings of the palaces; and all the genius of the masters, all the images and visions they have left upon canvas, seem to tremble in the sunbeams and dance upon the waves. That is the perpetual interest of the place—that you live in a certain sort of knowledge as in a rosy cloud." [5] The arts of Europe represented Europe not only in subject, in visual imitation, but in suggestion and evocation. The great old buildings, centers of architecture and of decoration, seemed to James particularly suggestive. In his biography of W. W. Story, for instance, he speaks of his feeling of "the palaces really having . . . more to say about everything Roman than any other class of object." [6] There a history and a way of life, the very society surrounding, are part of the esthetic interest. When the principal character of one of James' last unfinished novels, *The Sense of the Past,* quite literally enters the life of a former age by way of a London house, James was imaginatively restating one of his earliest impressions.

The human suggestiveness of the work of art was particularly great for James, for he stood in direct opposition to that sterile estheticism which attempts to distinguish the apprehension of beauty from the apprehension of greater values in the life of the human being. In an unpublished letter to his mother he once said of the great statue of Marcus Aurelius in Rome, "If to directly impress the soul, the heart, the affections, to stir up by some ineffable magic the sense of all one's human relations & of the warm surrounding presence of human life—if this is the sign of a great work of art—this statue is one of the very greatest." [7] The belief is closely related to his response to the Pitti Palace

4. Ibid., p. 137.
5. *Portraits of Places* (Boston, James R. Osgood & Co., 1884), p. 24.
6. *William Wetmore Story and His Friends* (2 vols. Boston, Houghton, Mifflin & Co., 1903), *1*, 360.
7. To mother, Nov. 21 [1869], in HL.

in Florence: "Chancing upon such a cluster of objects in Italy—glancing at them in a certain light, in a certain mood—one gets a sense of *history* that takes away the breath." [8] These great monuments of art were an embodiment of human life, and spoke to the mind and imagination as well as to the eye. For in all great art, as in the Palazzo Corsini in Florence, "the past seems to have left a sensible deposit, an aroma, an atmosphere." [9] By means of the arts life is caught, the past is made a part of the present, and continuity and tradition are made tangible.

Thus the arts, as James said of the châteaux of France, "appeal in this mystical manner to the retrospective imagination." [1] At their suggestion he could project his mind and imagination, not altogether playfully, into the life of the past, into the history which had formed the Europe which he knew. The Château de Blois, described at some length in *A Little Tour in France,* summed up for James this evocative quality, on which he scattered comments through his whole description: "As you cross its threshold, you step straight into the brilliant movement of the French Renaissance." [2] "The wide, fair windows look as if they had expanded to let in the rosy dawn of the Renaissance." [3] "Pass . . . into the court, and the sixteenth century closes round you." [4] "The place is full of Catherine de' Medici, of Henry III., of memories, of ghosts, of echoes, of possible evocations and revivals." [5] "The place is a course of French history." [6] Such a magnificent example might well stand as a symbol of all the European arts, and equally well as a symbol of the meaning of the arts for James, the meaning which contained in suggestion the history and the tradition of Europe.

In America, on the other hand, James found a symbol of the native arts in the great houses of the newly rich, and their most noticeable quality was just their lack of any suggestion of continuity or tradition:

> Unmistakably they all proclaimed it—they would have cost still more had the way but been shown them; and, meanwhile, they added as with one voice, they would take a fresh start as soon as ever it should be. "We are only instalments, symbols, stop-gaps," they practically admitted, and with no shade of embarrassment; "expensive as we are, we have nothing to do with continuity, responsibility, transmission, and don't in the least care what becomes of us after we have served our present purpose." [7]

8. *Transatlantic Sketches,* p. 313.
9. Ibid., p. 304.
1. *A Little Tour in France* (Boston, James R. Osgood & Co., 1885), pp. 41-2.
2. Ibid., p. 24.
3. Ibid., p. 27.
4. Ibid., p. 28.
5. Ibid., p. 29.
6. Ibid., p. 30.
7. *The American Scene* (New York and London, Harper & Bros., 1907), pp. 10-11.

America, of course, was capable of great art, and James pointed with pride to Sargent's portrait of Major Higginson at the Harvard Union: "Innumerable, ever, are the functions performed and the blessings wrought by the supreme work of art, but I know of no case in which it has been so given to such a work to make the human statement with a great effect, to interfuse a group of public acts with the personality, with the characteristics, of the actor." [8] Great art always, no matter what its native ground, had for him a suggestive quality in relation to the life about it. But American art in general seemed to have no relation with anything beyond its immediate surroundings.

Interestingly enough, James was more amused than hurt by this American quality: "Since every part, however blazingly new, fails to affect us as doing more than hold the ground for something else, some conceit of the bigger dividend, that is still to come, so we may bind up the aesthetic wound, I think, quite as promptly as we feel it open." [9] His amusement was greatest, perhaps, at the thought of Columbia University moving progressively farther up town: "It has taken New York to invent, for the thickening of classic shades, the 'moving' University; and does not that quite mark the tune of the dance, of the local unwritten law that forbids almost *any* planted object to gather in a history where it stands, forbids in fact any accumulation that may not be recorded in the mere bank-book?" [1] It is no wonder that, reminiscent of his remarks in *Hawthorne* on the qualities missing for the artist in American life, he could speak of the American artist as "gasping at home for vital air." [2]

Whatever his disappointment in American art, the contemporary European art was equally disappointing: "The flower of art in these latter years has ceased to bloom very powerfully anywhere; but nowhere does it seem so drooping and withered as in the shadow of the immortal embodiments of the old Italian genius. You go into a church or a gallery and feast your fancy upon a splendid picture or an exquisite piece of sculpture, and on issuing from the door that has admitted you to the beautiful past you are confronted with something that has all the effect of a very bad joke." [3] Europe for James had ceased to be the great workshop; "The old Italy has become more and more of a museum, preserved and perpetuated in the midst of the new." [4] Yet as a great museum, Europe enjoyed a tremendous advantage over America, for it possessed the art, still as great as when first created, and it possessed the tradition established and illustrated by the art, that tradition

---

8. Ibid., p. 58.
9. Ibid., p. 137.
1. Ibid., pp. 138–9.
2. *W. W. Story*, I, 9.
3. *Portraits of Places*, p. 44.
4. Ibid., p. 46.

which James found so important to his own sensibility. As he noted, watching a difficult copy of a Ghirlandaio being made, "The old painters are dead, but their influence is living." [5] Europe was still the living museum, and James could find inherent in its exhibits the evocations and the suggestions which were to play so large a part in the themes of his novels.

While first grappling with the art of the novel, however, James also played the part of a professional art critic, for during the period from 1870 to 1890 he published a number of critical reviews and articles in American periodicals. The earlier ones for the most part took the form of hasty reviews of current exhibitions in Boston, New York, and London, and were not subsequently collected or reprinted. Later criticism, during the eighties and even into the early nineties, appeared in essays of more "literary" character on particular artists or forms of art, and was reprinted in *Picture and Text* in 1893. Despite the ephemeral nature of most of this criticism, and the often shallow nature of the reviews, they do lead the reader to some understanding of James' esthetic principles. They are particularly indicative because of James' insistence on the necessity and the value of criticism of the arts. Throughout his own criticism he assumed its representative importance, and from time to time even added a few parenthetical words of defense. In the first part of the article, "On Some Pictures Lately Exhibited," in the *Galaxy* of July, 1875, he presented his longest and most carefully reasoned defense of the critics, particularly the literary art critics, and concluded of their work: "It talks a good deal of nonsense, but even its nonsense is a useful force. It keeps the question of art before the world, insists upon its importance, and makes it always in order." [6] James was always serious about art in any form.

Although he considered criticism of art important, he never placed criticism above art itself. In making the point, he almost contradicts his own defense: "Art is one of the necessities of life; but even the critics themselves would probably not assert that criticism is anything more than an agreeable luxury—something like printed talk." [7] Since criticism is "something like printed talk," however, and since his own criticism tends to be more descriptive than analytical or evaluative, his later remark on Charles Eliot Norton is particularly revealing: "His interest was predominantly in Art, as the most beneficial of human products; his ostensible plea was for the esthetic law, under the wide wing of which we really move, it may seem to many of us, in an air of strange and treacherous appearances, of much bewilderment and not a

---

5. *Transatlantic Sketches*, p. 278.
6. "On Some Pictures Lately Exhibited," *The Galaxy, 20* (July, 1875), 89.
7. "Contemporary Notes on Whistler vs. Ruskin," in *Views and Reviews* (Boston, Ball Publishing Co., 1908), p. 214.

little mystification; of terribly fine and complicated issues in short, such as call for the highest interpretative wisdom." [8] The bewilderment and mystification of art for James was compelling enough to forbid the formulation of an absolute and unalterable system of values for others; he preferred simply to recognize excellence by a sort of reasoned instinct, and then to enjoy it when he found it.

Over this method of genial appreciation he found himself at odds with Ruskin: "As for Mr. Ruskin's world of art being a place where we may take life easily, woe to the luckless mortal who enters it with any such disposition. Instead of a garden of delight, he finds a sort of assize-court, in perpetual session. Instead of a place in which human responsibilities are lightened and suspended, he finds a region governed by a kind of Draconic legislation." [9] He was more in sympathy with Walter Pater, possibly the best-known critic of the period, who wrote, "What is important . . . is not that the critic should possess a correct abstract definition of beauty for the intellect, but a certain kind of temperament, the power of being deeply moved by the presence of beautiful objects." [1] James agreed with the lack of necessity for abstract definition, and based his criticism upon the belief, although he did not entirely agree with the necessity for a certain kind of temperament, that indirect statement of Pater's principle of criticism, "to know one's own impression as it really is, to discriminate it, to realise it distinctly." [2] James never tried to give the emotional, interpretative, lyrical criticism of the sort exemplified by Pater, but rather hid his own emotional response behind a matter-of-fact description of the object at hand.

In an unpublished letter to his mother he defines two ways of looking at pictures: "One in which the mind demands simple unqualified pleasure & exaltation: the other critical considerate & questioning. The first is really much the more fastidious of the two & I fancy it to be well that it should find only occasional satisfaction. When the second is uppermost, almost any gallery is a very pleasant place." [3] The first was his own preference, in writing as in observation, and his remark, "Criticism is appreciation or it is nothing . . . ," [4] is his nearest approach to a definition of his critical methods. From his various appreciations, however, some knowledge of his general preferences may be gained, if not a reconstruction of an absolute system of values. Contradictions are numerous, and appreciation is often expressed in vague generalities or

8. "An American Art-Scholar: Charles Eliot Norton," in *Notes on Novelists; with Some Other Notes* (New York, Charles Scribner's Sons, 1914), p. 422.
9. *Portraits of Places,* pp. 68–9.
1. Walter Pater, Preface to *The Renaissance; Studies in Art and Poetry,* Collected Works (London and New York, Macmillan & Co., Ltd., 1900), *1,* x.
2. Ibid., p. viii.
3. To mother, Nov. 21 [1869], in HL.
4. *Picture and Text* (New York, Harper & Bros., 1893), p. 13.

in critical terms which defy exact definition, but in the criticism as one body certain unformulated standards for personal evaluation do inevitably appear.

In speaking of a number of Holbeins exhibited in London in 1879, James wrote, "The interest of this noble series of portraits . . . is that of all Holbein's work—a strong and incorruptible reality, a rendering of the individual outline, of the literal facts and idiosyncrasies of the face, that has never been surpassed." [5] The comment illustrates his first and most basic preference in painting, a close resemblance to the object portrayed. His demand was not for strict realism—when it came to photography he spoke of "that hideous inexpressiveness of the mechanical document" [6]—but rather for the "direct, independent, unborrowed impression" [7] which he found in the best work of John Singer Sargent. Clarity of vision he thought the first requirement of any artist, and then the ability to reproduce that vision manually. But the vision had to be a natural and an honest one: "Mr. Homer goes in, as the phrase is, for perfect realism, and cares not a jot for such fantastic hair-splitting as the distinction between beauty and ugliness. He is a genuine painter; that is, to see, and to reproduce what he sees, is his only care; to think, to imagine, to select, to refine, to compose, to drop into any of the intellectual tricks with which other people sometimes try to eke out the dull pictorial vision—all this Mr. Homer triumphantly avoids." [8] James had a sharp eye for "intellectual tricks," and could always catch the hint of dishonesty in a painter: he found Sir Joshua Reynolds' "Strawberry Girl," "more fondly mannered than critically real." [9] As a result, his praise was often as much for the avoidance of technical tricks as for the achievement of an immediate vision. He said of Edwin Abbey, for instance, "His drawing is the drawing of direct, immediate, solicitous study of the particular case, without tricks or affectations or any sort of cheap subterfuge." [1] A love of vivid reality and a hatred of intellectual tricks formed the foundation of his esthetic preference in painting.

To the modern eye, however, his strong preference sometimes led him astray. His lack of appreciation for Whistler provides the most glaring example:

> Mr. Whistler, it is known, is an "impressionist". . . . It may be good to be an impressionist; but I should say on this evidence that it were vastly better to be an expressionist. Mr. Whistler's productions are, in the very nature of the case, uninteresting; they belong

---

5. "The Winter Exhibitions in London," *The Nation, 28* (Feb. 13, 1879), 116.
6. "The Picture Season in London," *The Galaxy, 24* (Aug., 1877), 155.
7. *Picture and Text*, p. 114.
8. "Pictures Lately Exhibited," p. 93.
9. "The Bethnal Green Museum," *The Atlantic Monthly, 31* (Jan., 1873), 71.
1. *Picture and Text*, p. 56.

to the closet, not to the world. They may be good studio-jokes, or even useful studio-experiments, but they illustrate only what one may call the self-complacency of technicality. To people who stand on their two feet and look at a reproduction of life with their two eyes, they appeal with no persuasive force whatever."[2]

A dislike of Whistler, however, was only to be expected of James, knowing his basic preferences: "Mr. Whistler's experiments have no relation whatever to life; they have only a relation to painting."[3] In keeping, his preferences denied the French impressionists as well. By the end of his life James' opinion had changed somewhat, it is pleasing to note, and he could speak in *The American Scene* of "an array of modern 'impressionistic' pictures, mainly French, wondrous examples of Manet, of Degas, of Claude Monet, of Whistler, of other rare recent hands."[4] But throughout most of his life he was distrustful of impressionism, and generally took the opportunity to condemn it. His position is most clearly defined in a comment on Sargent's "El Jaleo," a painting which James considered a typical illustration of the new movement: "It looks like life, but it looks also, to my view, rather like a perversion of life, and has the quality of an enormous 'note' or memorandum, rather than of representation."[5] Any clouding or perversion of a clear, vivid, and complete view of reality, regardless of the theory behind it, made the art correspondingly less satisfactory.

James summed up his basic preferences when he said of a painting under discussion that "superficiality is the only vulgarity and the only immorality, and that to be broadly *real*, in any case, is to be interesting."[6] His admiration of the "broadly *real*" was only the solid foundation for preference, however, and in such critical comments as that on a portrait by Copley, "He was definite, as we say; but that adventurous vision of the indefinite which has brushed with its wing all the very greatest works of art is never reflected here,"[7] James shows his desire for something more than realism. The exact nature of this "something more" he never makes clear; he simply assumes understanding, as when he said of the little Dutch master Van der Helst, "In all his unmitigated verity you detect no faintest throb of invention blossoming into style and straggling across the line which separates a fine likeness from a fine portrait."[8] As he indicates there, however, at least part of the

2. "The Grosvenor Gallery and the Royal Academy," *The Nation, 24* (May 31, 1877), 320.
3. "Season in London," p. 156.
4. *The American Scene*, p. 44.
5. *Picture and Text*, p. 102.
6. "Boston," in "Art" column, *The Atlantic Monthly, 29* (Mar., 1872), 373.
7. ["Portrait by Copley"], *The Nation, 21* (Sept. 9, 1875), 166.
8. "The Dutch and Flemish Pictures in New York," in "Art" column, *The Atlantic Monthly, 29* (June, 1872), 759.

quality, and certainly one of the ways in which it showed itself, was personal style. Of one of Sargent's portraits he said, in a most ambiguous statement, but one of his few definitions: "The picture has this sign of productions of the first order, that its style clearly would save it if everything else should change—our measure of its value of resemblance, its expression of character, the fashion of dress, the particular associations it evokes. It . . . arouses even in the profane spectator something of the painter's sense, the joy of engaging also, by sympathy, in the solution of the artistic problem." [9] Style is the coloring given a keen vision, the indefinable personal quality which makes the observer as well as the artist a part of the creative process, and yet which indicates unmistakably the individual sensibility of the artist.

One of the components of style is apparent in his praise of Mrs. Spartali Stillman: "This lady is a really profound colorist; but the principal charm of her work is the intellectual charm—that thing which, when it exists, always seems more precious than other merits, and indeed makes us say that it is the only thing in a work of art which is deeply valuable." [1] One is free to find his own interpretation of the phrase, but "intellectual charm" seems to mean for James both the attraction of the art for the intellect of the observer, and the quality of thought, whether conscious or not, presented by the artist. In *Transatlantic Sketches* he could even say of Ghirlandaio, "He was not especially addicted to giving spiritual hints; and yet how hard and meagre they seem, the professed and finished realists of our own day, ungraced by that spiritual candor which makes half the richness of Ghirlandaio!" [2] In the comment on Sargent's style he speaks of "the joy of engaging also, by sympathy, in the solution of the artistic problem." This joy is the essence of the intellectual charm of art; it is the full appreciation of the amount of intellect superimposed on reality by the artist. As in the reading of James' novels, the observer must not relax into passive receptivity, but must contribute the necessary sympathetic intelligence evoked by the artist.

The successful engagement of the observer's intelligence did not, however, mean for James a direct pictorial statement of intellectual content. His position is perhaps best explained in a private letter on the beauty of Raphael's art: "I say its beauty—I mean its exquisite unutterable beauty. As regards meaning & character, religious feelings &c I don't believe there is much more in his work than the spectator himself infuses under the inspiration of the moment—the influence that descends from them & lifts him from the level of his common point of view." [3]

9. *Picture and Text,* pp. 97–8.
1. "Pictures Lately Exhibited," p. 91.
2. *Transatlantic Sketches,* p. 298.
3. To mother, Oct. 13 [1869?], in HL.

Similarly, neither did the engagement of the observer's intelligence mean for James the intellectual participation of allegory or implied narrative. He actively disliked explanatory art, and took many opportunities to condemn its prevalence among his contemporaries. As he said once of the Royal Academy, "The savor of aesthetic Philistinism is of the strongest; the pictures all seem painted down to the level of the most vulgar *bourgeois* taste. Everything is anecdotal; the sense of beauty, of form, of imaginative suggestiveness, is strikingly absent." [4]

There was one exception. For the art of illustration, one of the joys of James' own youth, he showed great appreciation, particularly in the essay reprinted under the title of "Black and White" in *Picture and Text*. But such pictures, making no pretense of self-sufficiency, were for James a craft apart from great art. They could find their intellectual charm outside of themselves, just as to some extent anecdotal or allegorical pictures could. Great art possessed the esthetic self-sufficiency of Frederick Leighton's statue, "Young Man Struggling with a Python": "It has that quality of appealing to our interest on behalf of form and aspect, of the plastic idea pure and simple, which is characteristic of the only art worthy of the name—the only art that does not promptly weary us by the pettiness of its sentimental precautions and the shallowness of its intellectual vision." [5] Intellectual charm might exist in many forms, but for James it was necessarily an integral part of the esthetic whole.

If intellectual charm was not to be found in direct statement or in an artificial anecdotal element, however, it might be present in the sheer fertility of the artist's creative imagination. James found it in the painting of Burne-Jones, giving that artist, above all other contemporaries, an admiration difficult to accept today:

> They are not only, beyond all comparison, the most brilliant work offered at present by any painter to the London Public, but they rank among the most eminent artistic productions of our day. It is possible to urge a hundred objections to them—to declare that they lack freshness and manliness, that they are affected, dilettantish, monotonous, unreal. They have an amount of imaginative force the mere overflow of which would set up in trade a thousand of the painters who are more generally accepted by the public. [6]

James knew well enough that Burne-Jones failed to show in his work the necessary clarity of vision and, in fact, violated all of his basic preferences: "It is the art of culture, of reflection, of intellectual luxury, of aesthetic refinement, of people who look at the world and at life not di-

---

4. "Grosvenor Gallery and Royal Academy," p. 321.
5. "Season in London," pp. 159–60.
6. "Grosvenor Gallery and Royal Academy," p. 320.

rectly, as it were, and in all its accidental reality, but in the reflection and ornamental portrait of it furnished by art itself in other manifestations; furnished by literature, by poetry, by history, by erudition." [7] Yet he freely forgave the faults for the sake of the vivid imagination.

A greater element of intellectual charm, however, and a component of style as well, was the suggestive and evocative quality which James found in art. Great art not only contained the quality of suggestion, it was great art because it contained the quality. As a sensitive traveler and observer, James in his letters and travel books and autobiographical reminiscences indirectly defined the quality and indicated his constant awareness of its presence; as an art critic he made it an accepted value for criticism, and one of the qualities of the arts most often praised. In *Picture and Text* there appears a compliment to Alfred Parsons which explicitly adds the quality to James' other preferences: "Half the interest of Mr. Parsons' work is in the fact that he paints from a full mind and from a store of assimilated knowledge. In every touch of nature that he communicates to us we feel something of the thrill of the whole —we feel the innumerable relations, the possible variations of the particular objects. This makes his manner serious and masculine—rescues it from the thinness of tricks and the coquetries of *chic*." [8] Faithfulness to nature, avoidance of tricks, and a full mind are all admirable qualities for the artist, but it is "the thrill . . . of innumerable relations" that makes his work true art. Without it, art is simply surface imitation, as James suggested when he said of Foxcroft Cole that his paintings lack "that lingering relish for something in objects over and above their literal facts. . . . It seems a great pity that a painter should ever reproduce a thing without suggesting its associations, its human uses, its general sentimental value." [9]

Since it is difficult to praise the suggestive quality of art without becoming analytical or without recounting, in the manner of Pater, all that is suggested, James usually contented himself with such general statements of admiration as his comment on two pictures by William Hunt: "Into each of these the very *genius loci* has been cunningly infused." [1] Only occasionally did he specify more exactly, as in his praise, built around a pun, of Crawford's huge statue of Beethoven in the old Hall of Music in Boston: "I recall vividly, from various scenes and occasions, . . . the effect of the great composer's image, . . . holding the note, guarding the idea, so to speak, of which the whole place was the expression." [2] The quality seemed particularly present in native

7. "Season in London," p. 157.
8. *Picture and Text*, p. 90.
9. "Boston," p. 372.
1. ["An Exhibition in Boston"], in "Art" column, *The Atlantic Monthly, 29* (Feb., 1872), 246.
2. *W. W. Story, I,* 317.

English painting. "I may frankly observe that English painting interests me chiefly, not as painting, but as English. It throws little light, on the whole, on the art of Titian and of Rembrandt; but it throws a light which is to me always fresh, always abundant, always fortunate, on the turn of the English mind." [3] Gainsborough's "Miss Boothby," for instance, "though sketchy as to everything but the face, is rich with the morality of all the English nurseries, since English nurseries were." [4] Such art led to something larger than the individual work itself: "Even if the pictures were better at the Academy, there would, to a visitor from another country, be something more interesting than their technical merit: I mean the evidence they should offer as to the English mind and character—the English way of thinking and feeling about all things, art included." [5]

James' nearest approach to a general definition of this evocative quality is contained in his discussion of W. W. Story's sculpture: "Story's work as a sculptor speaks, incontestably, of the public it had to confront and involves a view of that public. There are things in the arts, of a truth, that have more eloquence and value for us by that reference than they offer in any other way; so that positively, at moments, we find ourselves turn insistently from the work itself to the evoked spirit of its place and hour, which become, in its light, almost as concrete as itself." [6] This is the quality of reference, of evocation, of participation by the observer, for which James strove in his own work, and for which his criticism of art is so full of admiration. He noticed the element in any example of the arts, whether grand and formal or not, and his remark on a fine Veronese might serve to represent the lifelong admiration: "It is a complete and admirable specimen of the master; a broad, authentic, untarnished page from the book of Venetian glory." [7] This is the element which James employed in defining the themes of his novels, and it is the characterizing element of great art which he found in his own observations and in his formal criticism. There is a consistency and a basic esthetic taste there which draws the man, the critic, and the novelist more firmly into one unified being.

It is altogether fitting that such unity should be present, for although as an observer and as a critic of the arts Henry James presents a certain biographical interest, the interest is there primarily because he was a great novelist, and the literary critic is receptive to any knowledge which will increase his understanding of the mind of the author with

---

3. "London Pictures and London Plays," *The Atlantic Monthly*, 50 (Aug., 1882), 253.
4. "Bethnal Green Museum," p. 70.
5. "The London Exhibitions—The Royal Academy," *The Nation*, 26 (June 6, 1878), 371.
6. *W. W. Story*, 2, 80-1.
7. "Pictures Lately Exhibited," p. 97.

whom he is concerned. The ultimate goal is greater understanding of the literary products of that mind. In this particular instance the esthetic unity of James' mind makes the transition from the biographical to the critical interest, in so far as they can be separated at all, an easy one. Not only does he constantly echo his intimate knowledge of the visual arts in the novels, but he also makes extensive use of the arts to define and to illustrate the themes of his novels. It is in this use that the primary literary interest lies, for the visual arts, particularly in the light of the values which James himself found in them, provide a means of interpretation which is most helpful for the reader. The close relationship is particularly emphasized by the explicit analogy which James felt between the novel and the visual arts. In comparing the two in *Picture and Text* he said, "The forms are different, though with analogies; but the field is the same—the immense field of contemporary life observed for an artistic purpose. There is nothing so interesting as that, because it is ourselves; and no artistic problem is so charming as to arrive, either in a literary or a plastic form, at a close and direct notation of what we observe." [8]

Even a hasty glance at the prefaces to the novels reveals hundreds of extensions of the analogy, some much more specifically stated as matters of form and technique. James liked to use the vocabulary of the arts in discussing his own work, and regularly referred to a novel as "the picture" or "the canvas" or even "the embroidery," and to himself as "the painter" or "the artist." His concept of the novelist as artist in every sense is basic to his writing and his way of thought, and a necessary key to understanding of the man and his work. The idea is one to which another whole book might be devoted, for to James all great art eventually became one. But the formulation of an explicit analogy of the novel and the visual arts does provide an immediate link in theory, corresponding to the more important link in practice provided by the use of the arts within the novels, between James' criticism and observation of the visual arts and the art of the novel by which he wrote.

The analogy is one that might be discussed in detail, taking into account James' continual awareness of his full role of the artist, but in *The Art of Fiction* he offers a sufficiently lucid presentation of the analogy to point the way toward the fuller discussion which might be desired in other contexts. It is enough to say here that he finds many of the same values, in particular the evocative quality which conveys a sense of greater reference and wider suggestion in the single work. After defining the close correspondence, James was free to comment on the great possibilities open to the artist of either genre working within his own form and style. "The advantage, the luxury, as well as the tor-

8. *Picture and Text,* p. 65.

ment and responsibility, of the novelist, is that there is no limit to what he may attempt as an executant—no limit to his possible experiments, efforts, discoveries, successes. Here it is especially that he works, step by step, like his brother of the brush, of whom we may always say that he has painted his picture in a manner best known to himself." [9] What James himself achieved in the novel, and how that achievement may be apprehended through an understanding of the role of the arts in the novels, is the principal subject of this study. With a knowledge of his grounding in the visual arts, and with a knowledge of those critical preferences in the arts which he was to find so helpful in establishing his themes, it is time to turn to that more important consideration of James' own "experiments, efforts, discoveries, successes."

9. "The Art of Fiction," in Walter Besant [and Henry James], *The Art of Fiction* (Boston, Cupples, Upham & Co., 1885), p. 61.

2

The European-American Theme: Europe

THE visual arts provide a link between biography and literary criticism, but also, and certainly more important to the reader of Henry James' novels, provide a means of interpretation of the novels themselves. For James' novels, particularly his later ones, are alive with references to the arts. Often in the form of imagery and even symbolism, these references are seldom restricted in function to the simple establishment of scene and local color, or even to the strict definition of theme, but are an integral part of the greater structure and meaning of the novel. My interest, however, lies not so much in the manner in which James made use of the arts as in the understanding of the individual novel, and in particular the common themes of the novels, which that use offers. Since many of the novels are notoriously not easy or simple, it is critically useful to have in reading them some system of observation, a means of approach which leads directly to the center of the novel and there points the way to more detailed interpretation. The arts provide just such an approach, particularly in the light of James' own esthetic history, and offer just such an interpretation.

In chronology, in theme, and in style and method, James' novels fall easily into three broad groups, of which the first includes all but two of those published by 1888. That is, it is made up of *Roderick Hudson* (1876), *The American* (1877), *Watch and Ward* and *The Europeans* (1878), *Confidence* (1880), *Washington Square* (1881), *The Bostonians* (1886), and *The Reverberator* (1888). I have thought best to include *The Portrait of a Lady* (1881) and *The Princess Casamassima* (1886) in the next group to be considered in turn, but to add to the first the unfinished and posthumously published *The Ivory Tower* (1917), since it shows a return to earlier themes and interests. All of these novels make one group, for all are concerned to a greater or less degree with a definition of the distinguishing qualities of Europe and America. Many of James' novels make use of the "international incident," but only these are directly concerned with the placement of the European and American ethos, and with the distinctions to be made between the two civilizations. The references to the arts, although relatively fewer in these earlier novels than in the later ones, are an essential part of this common theme of international definition, and offer a critically valid means of approach.

To restrict the discussion of any of the novels to the usefulness of the arts in understanding James' themes, however, is to undervalue the method itself as well as James' particular art of the novel. The arts are frequently an aid to the understanding of plot and character as well, and lead the reader to a recognition of more minute and perhaps at times less important elements than the greater theme. To illustrate the full method, therefore, as well as to comment at greater length on some of the more interesting and rewarding novels, the discussion of the usefulness of the arts to the understanding of the particular theme of a group of novels will from time to time be broadened to include a demonstration of their usefulness to a more general interpretation of a complete novel. In the first group, for instance, *The American* and *The Europeans*, in the second group *The Portrait of a Lady* and *The Spoils of Poynton*, and in the third group *The Wings of the Dove* and *The Golden Bowl* offer particular interest beyond that of the unifying theme. So do many of the others, but the necessary economy of concentration demands a certain ruthlessness. It is hoped that the reader, given a more nearly complete discussion of a few novels, will in turn find the method useful for a full reading of those others to which it is applied here in a restricted or necessarily limited degree.

Roderick Hudson, the novel which James later wished accepted as his first, provides an excellent introduction to the interpretative value of the arts in the early novels, for in it James makes clear the role which the arts were to play with increasing emphasis through the novels yet to come. *Roderick Hudson* is at times fumbling and awkward, with a faulty grasp of character and situation; it is no wonder that James was later to call it, "a book of considerable good faith, but I think of limited skill." [1] Yet despite its faults, James maintains a careful control of the suggestiveness of the arts in the novel, particularly in the characterization. There is, for instance, a firmly established symbolism in which each of Roderick Hudson's sculptures defines one phase of the young sculptor's career. More subtly, his sculpture often suggests elements of his own character. The novel inevitably suggests Hawthorne's *Marble Faun*, even though James is not establishing an identification so explicit and static as that of Donatello and the Praxiteles statue.

The value of the arts for examining the characterization, however, unsatisfactory as that characterization may finally be, points even more directly in this novel as in others to the value of the arts for understanding the dominant theme of this early group, the definition of the European ethos, particularly in contrast to the American. From the moment Rowland Mallet suggests that Roderick as a student of sculpture must, as a matter of course, study in Italy, James characterizes Europe by continual reference to the visual arts. In Rome the two men

---

1. To R. L. Stevenson, Dec. 5 [1887], in *Letters, I,* 132.

seem to live in one tremendous gallery. Sculptures, pictures, sketches, buildings, public squares, galleries, cathedrals pass in confusing prodigality, and all mentioned with sure knowledge. By the middle of the novel one almost feels with Rowland the need for "a truce to present care for churches, statues, and pictures." [2] This preoccupation with the art of Europe goes far beyond the necessary "local color," for James is not intent on simply reproducing the Europe which he sees about him. Like the protagonist of his short story *The Real Thing,* he presents "an innate preference for the represented subject over the real one: the defect of the real one was so apt to be a lack of representation." [3] The arts of Europe, in fiction as in fact, represent for James a quality of life, gradually apparent in the novel, that is far more important than the arts themselves. To characterize this quality, he emphasizes so heavily—perhaps even so unrealistically—the arts in which it appears.

The American background, on the other hand, is singularly lacking in the arts, a lack which has an importance of its own. For *Roderick Hudson* is the first of the novels explicitly contrasting Europe with America, and in it America is to a great extent the land without art. It can produce artists like Roderick Hudson, of course, but they must go to Europe to study. And it can produce a natural taste for the arts, like the unspoiled Mary Garland, but she must go to Europe to feed that taste. To some degree, the novel is even a condemnation of America, one with which James never again completely agreed but which in this novel helps by contrast to make the esthetic value of Europe more striking. The plea for a native art, for instance, is early swept aside with casual irony in Roderick's patriotic outburst: "He didn't see why we shouldn't produce the greatest works in the world. We were the biggest people, and we ought to have the biggest conceptions. The biggest conceptions of course would bring forth in time the biggest performances. We had only to be true to ourselves, to pitch in and not be afraid, to fling Imitation overboard and fix our eyes upon our National Individuality." [4] It sounds like a parody of the genuine ideal of an Emerson, and the parody is complete when at the first offer of Italy Roderick immediately forgets his "National Individuality."

In this novel the common American taste is represented by Mrs. Hudson and Mr. Striker. (Mr. Leavenworth and his " 'allegorical representation of Culture' " [5] is entirely too Dickensian a figure to be taken seriously.) Mr. Striker, while scoffing at Roderick's desire to study the "antique" sculpture, makes the point for James: " 'An an-

---

2. *Roderick Hudson* (Boston, James R. Osgood & Co., 1876), p. 81.
3. "The Real Thing," in *The Real Thing and Other Tales* (New York, Macmillan & Co., 1893), pp. 11–12.
4. *Roderick Hudson,* p. 30.
5. Ibid., p. 174.

tique, as I understand it,' the lawyer continued, 'is an image of a pagan deity, with considerable dirt sticking to it, and no arms, no nose, and no clothing. A precious model, certainly!' " [6] The nakedness seems particularly to bother the good people of New England. Mrs. Hudson " 'has a holy horror of a profession which consists exclusively, as she supposes, in making figures of people without their clothes on. Sculpture, to her mind, is an insidious form of immorality.' " [7] In Italy the poor woman can only sit patiently, "looking shyly, here and there, at the undraped paganism around her." [8] Emerson's beliefs, embodied in the essay on *Art,* that art is essentially moral, since it is based on nature and suggests still higher forms and beings, commands little allegiance in this New England town of Northampton.

Within a still vital Puritan tradition of the compulsive seriousness of labor, the great arts are condemned not only as immoral but as mere decoration, mere idleness. The role of the artist is played in no traditional profession, and this is the greatest objection that Mr. Striker can make to Roderick's plans and hopes. Roderick may be " 'very enlightened, very cultivated, quite up to the mark in the fine arts and all that sort of thing,' " but Mr. Striker is " 'a plain, practical old boy, content to follow an honorable profession in a free country.' " [9] The feeling is widespread, and even Mary Garland, a girl with keen natural taste, feels that morally she must agree with Mr. Striker in her answer to Rowland's explanation of his plans:

> "I have the misfortune to be a rather idle man, and in Europe the burden of idleness is less heavy than here."
>
> She was silent for a few minutes; then at last, "In that, then, we are better than Europe," she said.[1]

And the irony of it all is that for Roderick at least she and Mr. Striker are right.

James quickly brushes aside the arts in America, for in this novel his interest is not in the definition of America but of Europe. America only provides contrast to the vast transatlantic museum. After noting that the Vatican takes on an added value by providing what the two men have been looking for, "the complete antipodes of Northampton," James goes on to say, "And indeed, Rome is the natural home of those spirits . . . with a deep relish for the artificial element in life and the infinite superpositions of history." [2] Rome represents age, represents

6. Ibid., p. 54.
7. Ibid., p. 27.
8. Ibid., p. 349.
9. Ibid., p. 58.
1. Ibid., p. 68.
2. Ibid., p. 84.

the accumulated weight of tradition bearing on the present. And this age, this weight, this tradition is caught in its art. James is agreeing in substance with Emerson that, "The whole extant product of the plastic arts has herein its highest value, *as history.*" [3] Rowland makes the concept clear in one of his conversations with the American Mary Garland:

> "Is *this* what you call life?" she asked.
> "What do you mean by 'this'?"
> "Saint Peter's—all this splendor, all Rome—pictures, ruins, statues, beggars, monks."
> "It is not all of it, but it is a large part of it. All these things are impregnated with life; they are the fruits of an old and complex civilization."
> "An old and complex civilization: I am afraid I don't like that."
> "Don't conclude on that point just yet. Wait till you have tested it. While you wait you will see an immense number of very beautiful things—things that you are made to understand. They won't leave you as they found you; then you can judge." [4]

This is the Europe of the "international situation," the Europe of the "infinite superpositions of history" which James himself had found. It is completely foreign to New England; it has immense depth and immense age to offer the modern life. And all this age, all beauty, all force, all tradition is present in its art.

The character of Roderick is profoundly influenced by Europe, and in the story Italy and all it stands for helps to bring about his final degeneration and death. His fiancée, Mary Garland, is affected even more sharply by her new life in Europe. At first she is perhaps too obviously " 'the fruit of a civilization not old and complex, but new and simple,' " [5] at least in comparison to the Europeanized Christina Light, of whom Rowland says, " 'It has taken twenty years of Europe to make her what she is.' " [6] But suddenly in Italy Mary begins to feel "the direct influence of the great amenities of the world, and they were shaping her with a divinely intelligent touch." [7] Taken from " 'corners where, perforce, our attitudes are a trifle contracted,' " [8] she all too quickly expands to full stature in the gallery of Europe. The effect is, in fact, that seen earlier, if only briefly, in Nora of *Watch and Ward:*

3. R. W. Emerson, "Art," in *Essays, First Series,* Centenary Edition (Boston and New York, Houghton, Mifflin & Co., 1903), p. 353.
4. *Roderick Hudson,* p. 305.
5. Ibid., p. 306.
6. Ibid., p. 170.
7. Ibid., p. 313.
8. Ibid., p. 313.

"It was as if she had bloomed into ripeness in the sunshine of a great contentment; as if, fed by the sources of aesthetic delight, her nature had risen calmly to its allotted level." [9]

This formative esthetic force of Europe, with its enlightening effect on the American mind, is well described by Mary, just beginning to shake loose the restricting and morally dogmatic education of New England:

> "I used to think . . . that if any trouble came to me I would bear it like a stoic. But that was at home, where things don't speak to us of enjoyment as they do here. Here it is such a mixture; one doesn't know what to choose, what to believe. Beauty stands there—beauty such as this night and this place, and all this sad, strange summer, have been so full of—and it penetrates to one's soul and lodges there, and keeps saying that man was not made to suffer, but to enjoy. This place has undermined my stoicism, but —shall I tell you? I feel as if I were saying something sinful—I love it!" [1]

In this poetry of expansion, of enlightenment, of renascence, she speaks for James' American in Europe.

Mary offers the fictional definition of the theme, although it wasn't until *The American* that James, carrying on the same thematic interest, fully exploited the definition. But in *The American* he embodied the theme so organically and so successfully in its dramatic illustration, the "international episode," that his many references to the arts provide a means of interpretation of the entire novel as well. Appropriately enough for the theme, the story opens with Christopher Newman, retired American businessman, in the great gilded "Salon Carré" of the Louvre—with an "aesthetic headache." [2] Even though "rather baffled on the aesthetic question," [3] he is thoroughly enjoying himself. Unlike the traditional American tourist, Newman shows little interest in "culture" for its own sake, and yet he shows equally little desire for coarse derision of it. Wealthy, confident, likable, but socially and culturally raw, questions are already beginning to form for him. "A vague sense that more answers were possible than his philosophy had hitherto dreamt of had already taken possession of him, and it seemed softly and agreeably to deepen as he lounged in this brilliant corner of Paris." [4] He knows clearly why he has come, certainly not from mental vacancy, and he has already begun to put his general plan for the fu-

---

9. *Watch and Ward* (Boston, Houghton, Osgood & Co., 1878), p. 127.
1. *Roderick Hudson*, p. 416.
2. *The American* (Boston, James R. Osgood & Co., 1877), p. 6.
3. Ibid., p. 8.
4. Ibid., p. 29.

ture into action: "'I have come to see Europe, to get the best out of it I can. I want to see all the great things, and do what the clever people do.'"[5] Even to Mr. Tristram, that vacant, worthless, and amusing American abroad, Newman has great possibilties.

Newman is ignorant of the arts, and has little or no taste. He admires the Veronese "Marriage-feast of Cana" because "it satisfied his conception, which was ambitious, of what a splendid banquet should be,"[6] just as he later admires his too ornate rooms because they satisfy his conception of what splendid rooms should be. He often admires the copy of a picture more than the original, and on a whim he sets out with characteristic directness to buy copies at any price. Even his choice of pictures to be copied by the unscrupulous and ambitious little Mademoiselle Nioche shows the same taste and the same desires as his choice of rooms:

> She gave another little shrug. "Seriously, then, you want that portrait—the golden hair, the purple satin, the pearl necklace, the two magnificent arms?"
> "Everything—just as it is."
> "Would nothing else do, instead?"
> "Oh, I want some other things, but I want that too."[7]

His taste in the other arts is no better, as James makes clear; "It is to be feared that his perception of the difference between good architecture and bad was not acute, and that he might sometimes have been seen gazing with culpable serenity at inferior productions."[8] At first glance it might seem that Newman is no more than a shocking example of the American esthetic atmosphere.

Yet despite his shortcomings Newman holds the sympathy of both author and reader, a direct contrast to Roderick Hudson whose taste is impeccable and whose character is despicable. Perhaps the explanation is to be found in the letter of Newman's traveling companion, the very moral and serious minister, Mr. Babcock: "'Art and life seem to me intensely serious things, and in our travels in Europe we should especially remember the immense seriousness of Art.'"[9] To take life or art so solemnly seems ridiculous to Newman; his life is far more relaxed.

> To expand . . . to the full compass of what he would have called a "pleasant" experience, was Newman's most definite programme of life. He had always hated to hurry to catch railroad trains, and

5. Ibid., p. 30.
6. Ibid., p. 19.
7. Ibid., p. 74.
8. Ibid., p. 84.
9. Ibid., p. 91.

yet he had always caught them; and just so an undue solicitude for "culture" seemed a sort of silly dawdling at the station, a proceeding properly confined to women, foreigners, and other unpractical persons. All this admitted, Newman enjoyed his journey, when once he had fairly entered the current, as profoundly as the most zealous *dilettante*.[1]

His lack of concern about taste allays the seriousness of his own lack. At the same time, his profound enjoyment of the journey through Europe removes him from the rank of those with no interest in art at all. His relegating a taste for the arts to women, foreigners, and other unpractical persons is familiarly American, but his own enjoyment of the arts takes the sting from the remark.

Newman retains sympathy too by making no pretence; he admits that he knows nothing about art. Yet he does know when Noémie Nioche is trying to take advantage of his "aesthetic verdancy."[2] He is, after all, nobody's fool. He simply knows his own limitations without feeling that he must hide them like Mr. Babcock or, even worse, boast of them like Mr. Tristram. And the culture of Europe does have its effect on him. After his summer of loafing about the continent, seeing the museums and the cathedrals and the sights, "He had done what he wanted; he had seen the great things, and he had given his mind a chance to 'improve,' if it would. He cheerfully believed that it had improved."[3] Without becoming a dilettante, and without surrendering any of his contempt for mere "culture," he comes to feel something of the strength of the artistic tradition of Europe, and so something of the essence of Europe itself. "It had come back to him simply that what he had been looking at all summer was a very rich and beautiful world, and that it had not all been made by sharp railroad men and stockbrokers."[4]

Christopher Newman, then, in the "international theme," represents the more admirable as well as the more undesirable qualities of the American in the old world. Despite his symbolic name, he is no obvious and mechanically defined symbol, and no "innocent abroad" in the sense of Mark Twain's scoffer. The very complexity and balance of his character is shown by his approach and response to the art of Europe. That Europe itself is characterized by this art is an accepted fact in the novel, and the shaping force of the tradition of the arts is constantly felt in *The American,* as in *Roderick Hudson.* Every chance reference to cathedrals and galleries and exquisite old homes makes the background an integral part of the story. Just as this tradition is

1. Ibid., pp. 82–3.
2. Ibid., p. 77.
3. Ibid., p. 93.
4. Ibid., p. 95.

taken for granted, the fact is calmly assumed that Valentin de Bellegarde, son of an old, old family, is a competent critic of art:

> She took up her little canvas and silently passed it to him. He looked at it, and in a moment she said, "I am sure you are a judge."
> "Yes," he answered, "I am." [5]

Within James' fictional world Valentin has inherited his taste just as he has inherited his background and his traditions.

In keeping with this quality of inherited feeling for the arts, some of the European characters are themselves even described in images drawn from the arts, as when Valentin likens Mademoiselle Nioche to " 'some little figure of a sea-nymph in an antique intaglio,' " [6] or when with precise placing of character by imagery Madame de Bellegarde reminds Newman of "a painted perfume-bottle with a crack in it," [7] and the marquis gives him "a sort of impulse to step backward, as you do to get a view of a great façade." [8] These people are the inheritors of the European tradition, are the products of that tradition, and something of its quality has entered into their very characters: "Madame de Cintré gave Newman the sense of an elaborate education, of her having passed through mysterious ceremonies and processes of culture in her youth, of her having been fashioned and made flexible to certain exalted social needs." [9] The result of this sympathetic fusion of character and background is that Newman and his circle of compatriots stand out in ironic relief against the background, and have a value and an identity marked by their American contrast to the European tradition.

There is no character in the novel, in fact, who is not presented, at least in part, with irony, often an irony conveyed by the arts. Perhaps the most obvious is the scheming little copyist, Mademoiselle Nioche. When she sells her copy of a young Madonna to Newman, she knows it is worthless, but as she says quite truthfully, " 'My copy has remarkable qualities.' " [1] Often the presentation even approaches the indirect comment of symbolism. One conversation between Newman and Mademoiselle Nioche clearly suggests such a view when read with reference to her character as it is known not at the time of the conversation but at the end of the novel:

> "But you must finish it," he said. *"Finish,* you know;" and he pointed to the unpainted hand of the figure.
> "Oh, it shall be finished in perfection; in the perfection of per-

---

5. Ibid., p. 187.
6. Ibid., p. 263.
7. Ibid., p. 268.
8. Ibid., p. 173.
9. Ibid., p. 152.
1. Ibid., p. 10.

fections!" cried mademoiselle; and to confirm her promise, she deposited a rosy blotch in the middle of the Madonna's cheek.

But the American frowned. "Ah, too red, too red!" he rejoined. "Her complexion," pointing to the Murillo, "is more delicate."

"Delicate? Oh, it shall be delicate, monsieur; delicate as Sèvres *biscuit*. I am going to tone that down; I know all the secrets of my art." [2]

As the novel progresses it becomes increasingly apparent that she does indeed know all the secrets of her art, although her art is not that of the painter, unless perhaps a painter of her own complexion.

Mademoiselle herself is only a copy of a Madonna, with too red a blotch painted on her cheek. She is intent on achieving success by her perfection of imitation, by her masquerading as a real lady. And then Newman "buys" this picture (to use a modern colloquialism), knowing full well that he pays too much for it, and yet not knowing until further events enlighten him just how bad a bargain he had made. This irony is continued through the course of the novel in the various references to the picture from the time of its delivery, hidden behind an inch of varnish and a foot-wide frame, and seeming to Newman "wonderfully splendid and precious," [3] to the moment of the remark by Noémie's father, "'It is almost a pity that her work is so perfect! It would be in her interest to paint less well.'" [4] By the time Newman watches her daub over another poor copy with a crimson cross and say, "'It is the sign of the truth,'" and then a moment later, "'Everything I have is for sale,'" [5] the reader is immediately able to catch James' complex intention.

Newman himself is not exempt from an irony that culminates in Mrs. Tristram's telling him, in the final agonizing twist of the novel, that the Bellegardes by ignoring his proof of their past crimes were not merely bluffing him, but were in reality taking advantage of his known character. For Newman, the shrewd, successful, American businessman, is accustomed to gaining his ends by rapid, straightforward means. "But," as James says, "Raphael and Titian and Rubens were a new kind of arithmetic, and they inspired our friend, for the first time in his life, with a vague self-mistrust." [6] He impetuously attempts to buy art before he understands it, and in the end he has not only made a poor bargain but has been cheated. The analogy to his hasty, direct, confident courting of Madame de Cintré, only to be cheated of her in the

2. Ibid., pp. 10–11.
3. Ibid., p. 59.
4. Ibid., p. 66.
5. Ibid., p. 189.
6. Ibid., p. 6.

end, is part of the ironic pattern of the novel introduced by his early comments on his worldly success: " 'I have succeeded, and now what am I to do with my success? To make it perfect, as I see it, there must be a beautiful woman perched on the pile, like a statue on a monument.' " [7] His attempt to buy Madame de Cintré, to place his own "marble goddess" [8] on top of the pile, provides the central situation of the novel.

In Brussels during Newman's first summer of travel, "he was ... greatly struck with the beautiful Gothic tower of the Hôtel de Ville, and wondered whether it would not be possible to 'get up' something like it in San Francisco." [9] The thought is typical of Newman, typical in fact of many American tourists busy bringing castles back to America, and is relevant to his attempt to take home Madame de Cintré, for it suggests his tendency, one which explains his lack of understanding of Parisian society, to dissociate objects and people from their surroundings and traditional background. In this sense he is indeed an innocent abroad, and James' description of him in the Preface as "some robust but insidiously beguiled and betrayed, some cruelly wronged, compatriot" [1] is only partially satisfactory. For Newman is not a simple victim; James makes it clear in the novel at least that Newman in his innocence and honest American directness is, ironically enough, partially responsible for his own failure.

In keeping with this fatal innocence, Valentin, a man of taste, smiles when he first sees the appallingly decorated apartment chosen to satisfy Newman's taste for obvious splendor:

> Newman looked at him a moment, and then, "So it *is* very ugly?" he inquired.
> "Ugly, my dear sir? It is magnificent." [2]

Both men, of course, are right, and Valentin's answer carries just the proper shade of ambiguity. For the apartment undoubtedly is magnificent even though it is not the right one for Newman. The ambiguity is pertinent, for it bears a strong likeness to the position of Newman himself who is admirable as a man but who is not fitted by taste or experience for the life of Europe, a life so closely paralleled by the arts of Europe. His final defeat springs from his failure to understand the inheritance of Europe, artistic or social, and this inheritance inexorably rules the Bellegarde family.

Much of this inheritance, for good and for evil, is suggested by the

7. Ibid., p. 48.
8. Ibid., p. 216.
9. Ibid., p. 81.
1. Preface to *The American,* Collected Novels and Tales (New York, Charles Scribner's Sons, 1907), 2, vi.
2. *The American,* p. 117.

surroundings of the Bellegardes, by their homes and furnishings and ornaments in which the feeling of great age is always suggested, the weight of tradition steadying and molding the present, generally in the form of some faded splendor of the past. The walls of the Paris house are "touched with long-faded gilding," [3] and the salon of the Marquise is vast and elaborate, "with a great deal of faded and carefully repaired tapestry in the doorways and chair-backs; a Turkey carpet in light colors, still soft and deep, in spite of great antiquity, on the floor." [4] The public reception room, fittingly enough, is even more suggestive of faded antiquity: [The chimney piece] "was of white marble, and in the familiar rococo style of the last century; but above it was a paneling of an earlier date, quaintly carved, painted white, and gilded here and there. The white had turned to yellow, and the gilding was tarnished. On the top, the figures ranged themselves into a sort of shield, on which an armorial device was cut. Above it, in relief, was a date—1627." [5] The smoking room, "ornamented with old hangings of stamped leather and trophies of rusty arms," [6] continues the impression, and even Valentin's separate little apartment is covered with "rusty arms and ancient panels and platters." [7]

This "Sense of the Past" in the European home—the allegorical values in the unfinished novel of that name are immediately applicable—is in direct contrast to the apartment of the Tristrams, the only American home in the novel. "Their apartment was rich in the modern conveniences, and Tristram lost no time in calling his visitor's attention to their principal household treasures, the gas-lamps and the furnace-holes." [8] The difference is particularly apparent when this "efficiency apartment" is compared with the Bellegardes' immense, dark, time-stained Henry IV château of Fleurières, that bleak and horror-filled château, so reminiscent of Poe's castles, which carries the feeling of age into the realm of romance, and emphasizes the romantic air of the later part of the novel.

This brooding age, this tarnished gilding and rusty armor of the past, is the element in which the Bellegardes exist, an element in which an American Newman, whose very name emphasizes his difference, cannot survive. Yet the Europeans are themselves so much a part of this element that the relationship, dramatized by the arts, may be exploited for ironic effect. One of the more obvious examples is the symbolic value given the "indifferent statue of an eighteenth-century nymph, simpering, sallow, and cracked," [9] which stands on the stairway of the

3. Ibid., p. 151.
4. Ibid., p. 167.
5. Ibid., pp. 107–8.
6. Ibid., pp. 199–200.
7. Ibid., p. 128.
8. Ibid., p. 35.
9. Ibid., p. 239.

Bellegarde home. It is twice mentioned, as if to call attention to itself, and at the second mention the reader suddenly recognizes its function: "The marquise and her two daughters were at the top of the staircase, where the sallow old nymph in the angle peeped out from a bower of plants. Madame de Bellegarde, in purple and fine laces, looked like an old lady painted by Vandyke; Madame de Cintré was dressed in white." [1] The statue is of a nymph of the age of elegance and artificiality and decorum with which the old Marquise likes to associate herself. But now it is sallow and old and cracked, like the Marquise herself. Madame de Bellegarde, like a Vandyke portrait, is another survival, but one with color and gaiety and life. Madame de Cintré, the pitiful victim of the European inheritance, is only a figure in white, the proper color for a sacrificial victim.

The social conventions and inheritances are presented with equal care, by a grimly humorous imagery of the arts, in the overtones of religious idolatry. Newman's introduction to the Duchess, the social leader of the old Parisian society, carries all of this force: "This little group had divided as the marquis came up, and M. de Bellegarde stepped forward and stood for an instant silent and obsequious, with his hat raised to his lips, as Newman had seen some gentlemen stand in churches as soon as they entered their pews. The lady, indeed, bore a very fair likeness to a reverend effigy in some idolatrous shrine. She was monumentally stout and imperturbably serene." [2] A reminiscence of the moment is found later in the description of a scene in Hyde Park: "Newman, as usual, marveled at the strange, dingy figures which he saw taking the air in some of the stateliest vehicles. They reminded him of what he had read of eastern and southern countries, in which grotesque idols and fetiches were sometimes taken out of their temples and carried abroad in golden chariots to be displayed to the multitude." [3] The leaders of society as religious idols; this, then, is the social inheritance of Europe, and this is now the true religion of the society of Europe. The frightening blank of the Carmelite convent in which Madame de Cintré is imprisoned, and "the grossly-imaged portals" [4] of Notre Dame are all that is left of the old beliefs and the old faith.

In the beginning of the novel Newman receives an ironic warning:

> "These," said Mr. Tristram, nodding at the Titians and Vandykes, "these, I suppose, are originals."
>
> "I hope so," cried Newman. "I don't want a copy of a copy."
>
> "Ah," said Mr. Tristram, mysteriously, "you can never tell. They imitate, you know, so deucedly well. It's like the jewelers,

---

1. Ibid., p. 273.
2. Ibid., pp. 277–8.
3. Ibid., p. 451.
4. Ibid., p. 468.

with their false stones. Go into the Palais Royal, there; you see 'Imitation' on half the windows. The law obliges them to stick it on, you know; but you can't tell the things apart." [5]

By the end of the novel Newman knows for himself the potential falsity of the life of Europe, and sums it up in answer to his housekeeper's plea that all his rooms are too gilded for her: " 'It's only tinsel, Mrs. Bread,' said Newman. 'If you stay there a while it will all peel off of itself.' And he gave a dismal smile." [6] In Newman's disillusionment, James had completed his preliminary definition of Europe, and was prepared to enlarge the theme to include the other side of the Atlantic as well.

5. Ibid., p. 22.
6. Ibid., p. 414.

3

The European-American Theme: America

BY the final pages of *The American* James had offered in some detail a definition of the European intellectual and social atmosphere and had explored the related problem of the American suddenly immersed in that atmosphere. Europe, particularly as it was dramatically illustrated in its arts, offered a life molded by a great tradition of the past, a life often deeper and more sensitive than the American, but also more corrupt and often more inhuman. The past was a great teacher, but a harsh and inflexible one demanding obedience without question or scruple. In James' early novels this Europe was to find its greatest expression in *The Portrait of a Lady,* a novel which seems more properly to belong to James' second, or middle, group. In the meantime James, possibly feeling that he had sufficiently exploited the European side of the international contrast, began to turn to the American side, although not without several weaker attempts to make use of his now familiar material. One attempt, *Confidence,* is by comparison a particularly poor novel. James later refused to recognize it, and in an unpublished letter to Constance Gardner commented amusingly on his refusal: " 'Confidence,' kindly believe me, is a very poor thing—I wholly disowned it in the definitive Edition; I mean kept it, with various other things, snubbingly out. So do I try to live down a shameful past—or at least one with shady episodes." [1]

Confidence is a shallow novel, not for what it accomplishes but for what it fails to accomplish. Given the story, James might have made of it a penetrating study of love and friendship, of conscience and guilt. But as it now stands it can only be called a hasty novel, Jamesian only in plot and international theme, with a commercially satisfying happy ending. One anticlimax follows another, a disappointing sequence easily seen by tracing the course of the artist's sketch which is made at the opening of the novel. It would seem that this sketch is to be a subject of some importance in the novel, and the means, like the golden bowl of the later novel or the nameless portrait of the short story *The Tone of Time,* by which the central characters are to make discoveries of the hidden relations between each other. Although this fictional device is carefully established, it is never used in *Confidence,* and the sketch, even brought back into the story several times, is al-

---

1. To Constance Gardner, Apr. 9, 1914, in HL.

lowed finally and disappointingly to drop from sight. The arts are present in the story, but are almost entirely decorative in function, emphasizing the surface quality of the novel itself. The background of Europe and its arts, although not at odds with the theme of the group, is little more than a painted backdrop before which the action takes place.

The novel is a poor one, but it has critical value in one respect, for it seems to indicate that James was tiring of the particular material of his earlier novels. In view of this apparent transition, it is interesting to look ahead to *The Reverberator,* although it was published some years later. For the little novel, light, gay and rapid, a sharp contrast to the "much more prodigious recitals," [2] approaches a parody of such novels as *Roderick Hudson* and *The American,* and so offers another indication of a shift in interests. The quality of parody is particularly apparent when *The Reverberator* is compared to *The American* where the concept of family unity and personal honor among the French is treated seriously indeed. There the inability of the aristocratic, European family of Madame de Cintré to accept her American lover is a matter of fine discrimination and grave seriousness. In *The Reverberator* the family of Gaston Probert is not old and aristocratic but recently arrived from America and trying hard to live like the aristocracy, and the inability of the family to accept his American fiancée is a matter of broad discrimination and gentle humor. The difference is essentially a matter of style and tone, for the theme has its same possibilities, and the situation is one capable of tragedy. But the Dosson family of the "Hôtel de l'Univers et de Cheltenham," and the Probert family (including Madame de Cliché) of the Place Beauvau are just a little too far apart to be believable: the Dossons too innocent and lost in Europe; the Proberts too self-conscious and representative of European social thought. The constant tone of slight exaggeration makes the novel a welcome comic variation of the weightier sober examination of the international theme.

The would-be European interest in the arts shown by the Probert family is never allowed to be taken seriously for long. James' method is to establish their general attitude toward the arts, and then with a momentary quirk of the eyebrow to slip in a remark which undermines completely any seriousness of intention: "The Proberts always fell into French when they spoke on a question of art." [3] It is seldom that James descends to more obvious humor to accomplish his purpose, although he is capable of it. While still intent on demolishing the European pre-

---

2. Preface to *The Reverberator; Madame de Mauves;* etc., Collected Novels and Tales (New York, Charles Scribner's Sons, 1908), *13,* vii.

3. *The Reverberator* (2 vols. London and New York, Macmillan & Co., 1888), *2,* 56-7.

tences of the Probert family, so suggestive of those of the Bellegardes, he can make one of its members, speaking of the portrait of Francie Dosson which plays such a large part in the novel, say that, "it might be a masterpiece of tone but it didn't make her look like a lady." [4]

Francie Dosson herself, like characters in *The American* or *The Portrait of a Lady,* is an example of the arts. She is her own best portrait, and she is a " 'charming object,' " [5] something to be appreciated only by a " 'sense of delicate things.' " [6] But the comparison, unlike that of the earlier novels, cannot be taken seriously. The inflated tone is immediately apparent in the enthusiasm of Gaston and the painter Waterlow over her pictorial qualities:

> The two young men, falling back upon their divan, broke into expressions of aesthetic rapture, declared that the girl had qualities—oh, but qualities, and a charm of line! They remained there for an hour, contemplating these rare properties in the smoke of their cigarettes. You would have gathered from their conversation (though as regards much of it only perhaps with the aid of a grammar and dictionary) that the young lady possessed plastic treasures of the highest order.[7]

The light irresponsibility in making the comparison can hardly be called accidental, for it is immediately apparent in the closing phrase of James' first introduction of Francie: "Mr. Dosson had not perhaps a full perception of his younger daughter's beauty: he would scarcely have pretended to judge of that, more than he would of a valuable picture or vase, but he believed she was cultivated up to the eyes." [8]

This form of humor, depending so much on slight exaggeration and unexpected introduction of the incongruous, is continued throughout the story and determines the tone of the novel as a whole. Its full effect is felt, however, only after a reasonable familiarity with James' more serious work. Just as some knowledge of James' use of the arts is necessary to recognize its parody here, so some knowledge of his definition of Europe and the "international situation" in such novels as *The American* is necessary to savor fully the parody of the theme in *The Reverberator.* That tone is again suggested by the use of the arts, and may be felt in the description of the Dossons' parlor at the "Hôtel de l'Univers et de Cheltenham": "They had, on the first floor, an expensive parlour, decorated in white and gold, with sofas of crimson damask; but . . . the place had become mainly a receptacle for their tall trunks, with a half-emptied paper of chocolates or *marron glacés*

4. Ibid., *2,* 56.
5. Ibid., *1,* 146.
6. Ibid., *1,* 148.
7. Ibid., *1,* 66.
8. Ibid., *1,* 37.

on every table." [9] Half-empty papers of chocolates in the midst of white and gold splendor carries just the proper hint of incongruity to characterize this notable example of the art of taking lightly, in retrospect at least, one's own serious efforts.

If *The Reverberator,* with its mocking glance at the first novels, and *Confidence,* with its shallow weakness, suggest in James a relaxation of interest in the European half of the international contrast, however, the other novels of this first group, *The Europeans, Washington Square, The Bostonians,* and even somewhat artificially added to the group, the posthumous fragment of *The Ivory Tower,* show a continuing interest in the American side of the theme. In one sense, *Washington Square* goes further toward a definition of the theme than the other novels, for there the formal arts, so representative of Europe, are hardly mentioned, and only the domestic arts given any noticeable attention. But the very absence has a strength of its own, for, as James had illustrated in *Roderick Hudson,* America within the international contrast is a land without art. Perhaps only in domestic architecture does it have a formal public art, and James accordingly limited his references. Painting, sculpture, or any formal art of long tradition would have denied the thematic contrast which the group as a whole makes.

The private houses of these novels, however, do offer again a means of interpretation. In *The Ivory Tower* the want of feeling among the completely American characters for anything beyond the tangible and the practical is echoed not only by a lack of interest in the formal arts, but by a very lack of taste in their houses, the one form of art which they cannot avoid. There is no need for James to draw obvious conclusions, he needs only to describe: "The nondescript excrescences of Gussy's 'cottage,' vast and florid, and in a kindred company of hunches and gables and pinnacles confessed, even if in confused accents, to its monstrous identity." [1] Wealth, pretentiousness, lack of taste, are all summed up in the description which echoes so directly many of the real houses of *The American Scene.* It is fitting that the final scene of the finished portion of the novel should be the sudden realization by Gray Fielder, the traveled and unrepresentatively sensitive young American, of the intense ugliness of the house he has inherited, an ugliness itself inherent in the American world of business wealth into which he is being forced: "He circled round the house altogether at last, looking at it more critically than had hitherto seemed relevant, taking the measure, disconcertedly, of its unabashed ugliness, and at the end coming to regard it very much as he might have eyed some

---

9. Ibid., *1,* 76.
1. *The Ivory Tower,* ed. Percy Lubbock (New York, Charles Scribner's Sons, 1917), p. 42.

monstrous modern machine." [2] "Monstrous" is the adjective applied to both houses, and it carries all the weight of ugliness and of latent danger, as though these houses and all they represent are about to devour Gray's finer sensibilities.

The houses of *Washington Square* make a similar contribution to an understanding of the theme. The old house of Dr. Sloper before his move to Washington Square, the "edifice of red brick, with granite copings and an enormous fan-light over the door," [3] emphasizes the solid abilities, combined with just enough elegance, which made him a success. But the new house in Washington Square, the house which dominates the novel, offers a more tangible quality. It suggests most obviously the sheer physical and economic success of the Doctor, a man who has taken his well earned wages—and high ones, too. "The ideal of quiet and of genteel retirement, in 1835, was found in Washington Square, where the Doctor built himself a handsome, modern, wide-fronted house, with a big balcony before the drawing-room windows, and a flight of white marble steps ascending to a portal which was also faced with white marble." [4] So much is straightforward enough, but in the next sentence the symbolic similarity of the Doctor and his house is made explicit with a certain grim irony: "This structure, and many of its neighbors, which it exactly resembled, were supposed, forty years ago, to embody the last results of architectural science, and they remain to this day very solid and honorable dwellings." [5] As the twisted mind of Doctor Sloper slowly becomes apparent under his sober and honest exterior, the irony of the description of his house increases until, with its reference to the neighboring houses, it seems almost a condemnation of a whole class of men.

The similarity between Doctor and house, ironic though it may be, is one the Doctor would approve. For despite his inner ferocity, the secret enjoyment of his active domination of his daughter, he likes to think of himself as "solid and honorable." It is no wonder that the worthless Morris Townsend, refused by him as a suitor for his daughter Catherine, sees in the entrance "the closed portal of happiness." [6] For to Morris the house represents all the wealth and position of the family which he is so desperately determined to seize for himself. "He thought it a devilish comfortable house." [7] Morris' one moment of petty triumph, fittingly enough, comes when he can steal into the doctor's own room while its owner is away. For the winning of that room, with its great easy chair and its sliding mahogany doors with silver fittings, seems

2. Ibid., p. 266.
3. *Washington Square* (New York, Harper & Bros., 1881), p. 22.
4. Ibid., p. 23.
5. Ibid., p. 23.
6. Ibid., p. 126.
7. Ibid., p. 127.

to him a symbol of the winning of the wealth and comfort and outward respectability which it represents. The moment is in many respects the turning point of his fortunes, for through the course of the novel his progression from one part of the house to another—the formal public rooms, the private study of Dr. Sloper, back to the public rooms, and at last down the steps never to return—is the curve of his fortunes in the novel.

Less explicit but equally helpful in interpreting both the American theme and the particular story of *Washington Square,* the symbolic value of dress and of American domestic art is carefully stressed. Catherine can express her character only in her "lively taste for dress," [8] unformed taste though it is. "Her great indulgence of it was really the desire of a rather inarticulate nature to manifest itself; she sought to be eloquent in her garments, and to make up for her diffidence of speech by a fine frankness of costume." [9] With such knowledge offered the reader directly, her crimson party gown takes on a meaning entirely missed by the ironic Dr. Sloper, for it looks forward by its suggestion of a bright and emotional nature to Catherine's silent, impassioned struggle to come. Then too, Catherine's domestic art helps to define the theme as well as to illustrate the deep struggle going on behind her quiet surface. And again, as with the dress, her father misinterprets or fails to understand this work.

After Morris has finally abandoned Catherine, and she is beginning to recover from the blow, Dr. Sloper says, "'She is perfectly comfortable and blooming; she eats and sleeps, takes her usual exercise, and overloads herself, as usual, with finery. She is always knitting some purse or embroidering some handkerchief, and it seems to me she turns these articles out about as fast as ever.'" [1] His callous and self-satisfied vision cannot see the meaning of this domestic art to her, the meaning made clear in the last chapter of the novel. For that chapter begins with Catherine seating herself "with a morsel of fancy-work," [2] and ends, after her final and complete rejection of the scheming but attractive Morris, with a telling sentence: "Catherine, meanwhile, in the parlor, picking up her morsel of fancy-work, had seated herself with it again—for life, as it were." [3] This slight art, this "morsel of fancy-work," represents for Catherine self-control and acceptance of her lot. She has undergone her silent and private tragedy, has exerted the full moral strength of her will, and now must content herself with expression in an accepted, solitary manner. The art is both her defeat and her triumph.

8. Ibid., p. 20.
9. Ibid., pp. 20–1.
1. Ibid., p. 241.
2. Ibid., p. 256.
3. Ibid., p. 266.

THE EUROPEAN-AMERICAN THEME: AMERICA

The long trip to Europe on which Dr. Sloper takes Catherine to make her forget Morris Townsend gives James a chance—it would not do in America—to make some use of the more formal arts. Yet the use made is only to define character even further, and, fittingly enough, not at all to define America, or even Washington Square. Mrs. Penniman, the dramatic egotist who stays at home, makes it clear that art means nothing to her, although she will pay it the required lip service: " 'I should enjoy seeing the works of Raphael and the ruins—the ruins of the Pantheon,' she said to Mrs. Almond; 'but, on the other hand, I shall not be sorry to be alone and at peace for the next few months in Washington Square.' " [4] She is far too interested in herself and her role in the events about her to be interested in art, vague and distant and foreign as it is. The American Washington Square is as large a frame of reference as she needs.

To Dr. Sloper too the enlarging possibilities of the trip are of no genuine consideration, and are completely apart from his true reason for leaving America. His excuse for staying longer than planned is heavy with irony: "He made the grand tour of Europe, travelled in considerable splendor, and (as was to have been expected in a man of his high cultivation) found so much in art and antiquity to interest him, that he remained abroad, not for six months, but for twelve." [5] To an American of such solidity and honesty, with a turn for cold observation, the arts are of no practical value beyond the social. In his usual sarcastic manner he recognizes this practical value, and employs it to torment his daughter: " 'I have done a mighty good thing for him [Morris] in taking you abroad; your value is twice as great, with all the knowledge and taste that you have acquired. A year ago, you were perhaps a little limited—a little rustic; but now you have seen everything, and appreciated everything, and you will be a most entertaining companion. We have fattened the sheep for him before he kills it.' " [6] Despite his bitter humor, it is interesting that he does notice in her an effect of the European voyage, even though he scorns it. One wonders what Catherine thinks.

Dr. Sloper tells Mrs. Penniman's sister that the trip had no effect: " 'Exactly the same; not a grain more intelligent. She didn't notice a stick or a stone all the while we were away—not a picture nor a view, not a statue nor a cathedral.' " [7] Her conduct on the trip would seem to bear this out, yet the report suggests again that Catherine's one defense in her tragic predicament is the cultivation of docility and inscrutability. Caught between a powerful father acting for her best in

---

4. Ibid., p. 168.
5. Ibid., p. 173.
6. Ibid., pp. 181–2.
7. Ibid., p. 201.

the cruelest manner, and a lover acting for her worst in the most charming manner, Catherine can only draw further into her protective shell of apparent passivity. She is not unresponsive; she is highly sensitive. Perhaps her outer response to Europe, potentially as indicative for the theme of these novels as that of Mary Garland in *Roderick Hudson,* is like her dependence upon the domestic arts, another secret means of covering her inner feelings, another method of circumventing the force of her father.

Her deliberate withdrawal into a private world untouched by the larger one abroad, however, is thematically representative: America is itself a narrow world untouched by the larger one abroad. But its intellectual narrowness is by no means geographical narrowness, as James was to find by experience in his later trip across the country, and clear variations in intellectual atmosphere as well existed even within the guarded borders. In *The Bostonians* James makes use of this intellectual variety in unity for his own thematic purposes. By establishing distinctions between sections of the one country—Boston, New York, the South—rather than between continents, he takes advantage both of the expansive quality of large contrasts, as in *Roderick Hudson* or *The American,* and the concentrated quality of limitation of locale, as in *Washington Square.* Like *Washington Square* too, the various characters of *The Bostonians,* with the exception of the Burrages, representing a cosmopolitan New York society, have little to do with the arts. But unlike *Washington Square,* where only the absence of the arts is stressed, *The Bostonians* is careful to comment upon the relative degree of absence or presence in the widely differing American societies.

A lack of interest in the arts in James' Boston is not surprising, for this society of inherited conscience, reminiscent of the Wentworth family in *The Europeans,* carefully avoids anything so light and worldly. To the inheritors of the Puritan tradition, in James' mind at least, only duty and conscience could be the arbiters of taste. Miss Chancellor, the representative of the old Boston society, believes that the study of esthetics or the development of an esthetic taste for its own sake is without meaning, and even borders on the frivolous and culpable. She early defines her own interest: "Taste and art were good when they enlarged the mind, not when they narrowed it." [8] Not unlike Catherine Sloper, her very narrowness, her intense aridity cultivated by a lifetime of moral self-control, despite her warped inner passions, her desire for love and control of others, forbids the arts to her. Ultimately this rejection is a matter of moral choice, of conscious and conscientious decision, rather than of any simple lack of interest. In her relation to the arts, as well as in the plot itself, she represents in

8. *The Bostonians* (London and New York, Macmillan & Co., 1886), p. 149.

the novel the strict New England conscience, a moral strenuousness in which the arts have no place.

In contrast to Olive Chancellor and such representative friends as Miss Birdseye stands the family of Henry Burrage, the dilettante, cosmopolitan, traveler, man of "enlarged mind" in the esthetic sense rather than in Miss Chancellor's moral sense. He is, perhaps, too hastily presented and too quickly forgotten in the novel, but when present he is seldom mentioned without some one of the visual arts being also mentioned. His rooms are rich with works of art, and at his mother's New York home, representing his own inherited tradition, "the walls of the room were covered with pictures—the very ceiling was painted and framed." [9] Naturally enough, he takes Verena into the "picture-room" [1] to speak to her during his courtship, and to the museum to amuse her—where she wonders at his "acquaintance with everything it contained." [2] His mother, Mrs. Burrage, with the same developed taste, talks to the troubled Olive "in a remarkably pretty boudoir, where there were flowers and faiences and little French pictures." [3] His very way of life and thought, so different from that of Boston, is characterized by means of the arts: "He collected beautiful things, pictures and antiques and objects that he sent for to Europe on purpose, many of which were arranged in his rooms at Cambridge. He had intaglios and Spanish altar-cloths and drawings by the old masters. He was different from most others; he seemed to want so much to enjoy life, and to think you easily could if you would only let yourself go." [4] Miss Chancellor does not want to enjoy life in that manner, she wants to be useful in life, and her method is not to let herself go, but increasingly to tighten the control of her will.

Basil Ransom, the young Mississippian, stands somewhat outside of this sharp contrast, for his role is that of the intruder into the scene. Like Miss Chancellor, he too is without a taste for the arts, not as a matter of conscience, however, but of ignorance. He is not without a vague aspiration for taste and appreciation but he makes no active move toward attaining them. "Basil Ransom had seen very few pictures, there were none in Mississippi; but he had a vision at times of something that would be more refined than the real world, and the situation in which he now found himself pleased him almost as much as if it had been a striking work of art." [5] In many ways he is like Christopher Newman in *The American:* a man with no particular

9. Ibid., p. 248.
1. Ibid., p. 253.
2. Ibid., p. 286.
3. Ibid., p. 303.
4. Ibid., p. 147.
5. Ibid., p. 359.

knowledge of art or interest in an artificial culture, but a willingness to take an interest if the occasion arises and promises sufficient amusement. But Newman is in Europe where the occasion arises every day, and Ransom is in America where the occasion must be sought. Like Newman too, Basil Ransom, despite his lack of worldly success and despite his occasional Mississippian longing for something outside of the "real world," represents the practical, realistic, rough man, here intruding upon and disrupting the world of the New England conscience. He is in many ways a representative of the greater America, as distinct from the small Bostonian group of a rather admirable Puritan morality, and the even smaller, and perhaps not so admirable, cosmopolitan, cultured, New York group. The arts to him are neither something to be sought nor something to be avoided, but merely a distant and relatively unimportant concept.

Through this representative divided society walks the original Verena Tarrant, a character not to be the subject of regional discriminations and not to be placed by her relation to the arts, but rather to be viewed herself as a work of art. Fittingly enough, Henry Burrage sees her as such: "The furthest he had gone as yet was to tell her that he liked her for the same reason that he liked old enamels and old embroideries; and when she said that she didn't see how she resembled such things, he had replied that it was because she was so peculiar and so delicate." [6] His statement is additionally, of course, an ironic comment on Henry himself, a man who sees only with the esthetic sense. It would be difficult to imagine Basil Ransome even thinking such a thing, and to Olive Chancellor the thought would have been almost sacrilegious. Yet even Olive finds something of that quality, seen not as the created but as the creator: "For her scrutinising friend Verena had the disposition of the artist, the spirit to which all charming forms come easily and naturally." [7] Verena is representative of nothing but herself, and her tragedy is to be found first in her attempt to live sympathetically with Olive, to join the restricted world of the conscience by rational effort, and then finally to surrender to the pleas of the realist, Basil Ransom, and to be torn from Olive's world to the hard practical world to which she no more rightfully belongs than to Olive's. With her original and natural charm she is like a beautiful work of art given first to one who will not appreciate it, and then to one who cannot. Only Henry Burrage, the one lover of art, might have saved her, but he is too weak, too much the dilettante, too much the esthete only, to be effective in this America of powerful, conflicting forces.

It is only occasionally in *The Bostonians* that James, although faithful to his international contrast, allows himself to castigate his country

6. Ibid., p. 148.
7. Ibid., p. 115.

as a whole as severely as he does individuals, but at those times, as later in *The American Scene,* the feeling seems too great to repress. His description of one character's room, "the big, hot, faded parlour of the boarding-house in Tenth Street, where there was a rug before the chimney representing a Newfoundland dog saving a child from drowning, and a row of chromo-lithographs on the walls . . . ,"[8] for instance, or his impression of Sixth Avenue and its "beer-saloons, with exposed shoulders and sides, which in New York do a good deal towards representing the picturesque, the 'bit' appreciated by painters,"[9] shows the mood clearly enough, particularly when compared with his early descriptions of Europe in nearly any one of his travel books. It is interesting that the only public work of art which James twice stresses in the novel[1] is the portrait of Verena on the lecture advertisements in shops and on fences all over town. This portrait not only emphasizes her quality as an object of appreciation, and the necessary public gaze to which she is not unwillingly subjected, but also helps to define the most popular taste for the arts in America.

With this popular taste so firmly established in his own mind as, for various reasons, good and bad, the representative taste of America, even though he refused to simplify the view to one of total ignorance of the arts, it was inevitable that James would use the comparison with Europe for thematic and dramatic conflict in his novels. And it was equally inevitable that after portraying the American in Europe he would turn to the European in America, a variation on the same theme. *The Europeans,* one of his notable early successes which deserves fuller treatment here, provides the example, and one of which he could be proud. With the story placed in New England, and the the old New England Wentworth family providing one of the two sets of major characters, James gives himself an opportunity to portray the New England scene and the New England mind. By also introducing to the family the Wentworths' very European cousins, Felix Young and his sister Eugenia, Baroness Münster, he is able to show the thematic contrast to this American scene.

The novel opens with Felix Young, the central character, sketching the Boston street scene. Like Roderick Hudson he is an artist, and therefore doubly a foreigner in the New England atmosphere. Unlike Roderick, however, his warm, careless, likable character, and his very frivolousness, supporting himself "by knocking off a flattering portrait of his host or hostess,"[2] provides an even greater contrast to his surroundings and particularly to the solemn Wentworth family. He and

---
8. Ibid., p. 279.
9. Ibid., p. 339.
1. Ibid., p. 320 and p. 419.
2. *The Europeans* (Boston, Houghton, Osgood & Co., 1879), p. 107.

his sister bring to the novel, in their relative degrees, the explicit European comparison. But Felix is also the reflector, the observer, the commentator. For although James' "reflector technique" is not as yet highly developed nor consistently followed, the events of the novel are seen for the most part through Felix' eyes. With the observer possessing a painter's way of thought and a painter's vivid pictorial sense, it is not surprising that the various references to the visual arts provide for the reader too such a convenient system of observation, an immediate means of interpretation of the novel.

In keeping with such interpretation, as well as with James' characteristic method in these early novels, the Wentworth family, solidly set in New England, is characterized by its house, just as the contrast offered by the Baroness is made stronger by the manner in which she redecorates the little New England cottage given her by the Wentworths. Like the Bellegarde mansion in *The American* or Dr. Sloper's house in *Washington Square,* the Wentworth house has an almost symbolic function. "It was an ancient house—ancient in the sense of being eighty years old; it was built of wood, painted a clean, clear, faded gray, and adorned along the front, at intervals, with flat wooden pilasters, painted white." [3] It is a "great, square, hospitable house," [4] a house, " 'lighter inside than it is out,' " [5] which has many of the characteristics of the Wentworths themselves. For this American family too, whose "sense of responsibility . . . constituted its principal furniture," [6] is large, clean, hospitable, solid, even a little gray, and with, figuratively, its own row of white columns. Its characteristic is not prettiness, certainly not beauty for its own esthetic worth, but the beauty of a stern sense of appreciation for honesty, for age—in America—and for wealth carried without ostentation or visible pride. Throughout the novel this solid, clean, clear, gray, New England house looms as an enormous and pervasive image.

Through Felix at least, the representative quality of the house slowly becomes more explicitly stated. To his sensitive eye the house has from the beginning something of the admirable quality of its family, even though his first impression is partly one of amusement:

> "There's a big wooden house—a kind of three-story bungalow; it looks like a magnified Nüremberg toy. There was a gentleman there that made a speech to me about it and called it a 'venerable mansion;' but it looks as if it had been built last night."
> "Is it handsome—is it elegant?" asked the Baroness.
> Felix looked at her a moment, smiling. "It's very clean! No

3. Ibid., p. 24.
4. Ibid., p. 251.
5. Ibid., p. 37.
6. Ibid., p. 67.

splendors, no gilding, no troops of servants; rather straight-backed chairs. But you might eat off the floors, and you can sit down on the stairs." [7]

He immediately senses its esthetic and moral value. But to Eugenia, whose mind never grasps the beauty of the very simplicity and lack of ostentation, the house remains forever a bungalow, a symbol not of the family's solid worth but of its lack of proper splendor and "ton."

To show these provincials how a house should look, and so indirectly to show much of her own character, Eugenia redecorates her own little house, originally small and white and typical of New England, in the dark, cluttered, ornate fashion of her Europe of the day. As her maid Augustine says, " 'Il faudra . . . lue faire un peu de toilette,' " [8] and the two go to work in their best style. "There were India shawls suspended, curtain-wise, in the parlor door, and curious fabrics . . . tumbled about in the sitting-places. There were pink silk blinds in the windows, by which the room was strangely bedimmed; and along the chimney-piece was disposed a remarkable band of velvet, covered with coarse, dirty-looking lace." [9] To young Gertrude Wentworth, beginning to awaken with an amusing start to horizons beyond New England, the prospect of such furnishings had been fascinating: " 'It will be very interesting. It will be a place to go. It will be a foreign house.' " [1] The finished house, as an example of the foreign and the exotic, lives up to her fondest hopes: " 'What is life, indeed, without curtains?' she secretly asked herself; and she appeared to herself to have been leading hitherto an existence singularly garish and totally devoid of festoons." [2] The sensible Charlotte Wentworth in the meantime, "had been on the point of proposing to come and help her put her superfluous draperies away." [3]

The only polite remark which the Baroness can summon for the Wentworth house is a stammered inanity which means nothing to the family: " 'I see you have arranged your house—your beautiful house—in the—in the Dutch taste!' " [4] For the only house in the neighborhood which the Baroness can honestly admire is that of Mr. Acton, the would-be man of the world:

> It was . . . a much more modern dwelling than Mr. Wentworth's, and was more redundantly upholstered and expensively ornamented. The Baroness perceived that her entertainer had ana-

7. Ibid., pp. 46–7.
8. Ibid., p. 80.
9. Ibid., p. 80.
1. Ibid., p. 72.
2. Ibid., p. 81.
3. Ibid., p. 80.
4. Ibid., p. 57.

lysed material comfort to a sufficiently fine point. And then he possessed the most delightful *chinoiseries*—trophies of his sojourn in the Celestial Empire: pagodas of ebony and cabinets of ivory; sculptured monsters, grinning and leering on chimney-pieces, in front of beautifully figured hand-screens; porcelain dinner-sets, gleaming behind the glass doors of mahogany buffets; large screens, in corners, covered with tense silk and embroidered with mandarins and dragons.[5]

This is what a house should be, consumption conspicuous enough to please the most ambitious of women, and a goal toward which a baroness with an eye on the main chance can move. " 'Comme c'est bien !' she said to herself; such a large, solid, irreproachable basis of existence the place seemed to her to indicate." [6] The obvious splendor, of course, blinds her to the "large, solid, irreproachable basis of existence" which the Wentworth house does in reality present.

The house of chinoiseries throws light not only on the Baroness, with her questionable if modern taste and motives, but also on Robert Acton. His favorite pose since a highly profitable trip to China is that of the traveled man of the world. Yet he is still essentially of New England, and must balk at the social lies of the Baroness. His New England conscience, like his New England house, may be filled with chinoiseries, but the original structure still shows through. Something of a dilettante in the arts, Mr. Acton knows a good deal about Chinese porcelains and bric-a-brac, and is very fond of pictures, "but it must be confessed, in the fierce light of contemporary criticism, that his walls were adorned with several rather abortive masterpieces." [7] Such a confused taste is typical of the man who is capable of a New England moral response to the Baroness, and yet is equally capable of using that response simply as an easy means of avoiding the marriage which he does not want. His is a mind only half formed on any model, and morally as well as esthetically it has no consistency of its own.

Mr. Brand, on the other hand, the ecclesiastical friend of the Wentworth's, and almost a member of the family, is a man whose solid, moral consciousness can drive him to acts of mental heroism. With a deliberate forthrightness he admits to Felix that he knows nothing about art, and in keeping with his moral training, like Mrs. Hudson in *Roderick Hudson,* he shies noticeably at several of Felix' pictures which in the gloom seem to represent naked figures. To Mr. Brand, as to the Wentworth family, art as such is suspect; Mr. Wentworth would rather refer to his nephew as an "amateur" than as an "artist," and in his own

5. Ibid., p. 131.
6. Ibid., p. 234.
7. Ibid., p. 116.

house has only maps, specimens, and "old-fashioned engravings, chiefly of scriptural subjects, hung very high." [8] Something of the Puritan suspicion of art still clings to Mr. Wentworth; he even questions the right of the artist to draw the human head; " 'The Lord made it,' he said. 'I don't think it is for man to make it over again.' " [9] He will have no idols and images about him; his children have his daguerreotype, and that is quite sufficient.

To a family for whom duty is the highest measure of conduct, and esthetic pleasure for its own sake is unthinkable, art has no place in the scheme of moral values, and so no place in life itself. "To consider an event, crudely and baldly, in the light of the pleasure it might bring them was an intellectual exercise with which Felix Young's American cousins were almost wholly unacquainted, and which they scarcely supposed to be largely pursued in any section of human society." [1] Yet this matter of esthetic taste and interest is neither so simple nor so clearly defined as it might seem, and leaves ample room for James' ironic comment. The Wentworth family, for instance, is admirable and honest and sound, yet its lack of any feeling for the arts goes beyond simplicity to a definite cultural lack, representative, it would seem, of the country itself. One may admire them for the moral strength behind this limitation, but the limitation itself remains. Gertrude, the rebel member, in breaking away from the family and yearning for a more complete life shows a laudable desire for esthetic and cultural enlargement which is in no sense lessened by such comic elements as her appreciation of the Baroness' festoons. Eugenia herself is morally unsound, and yet James makes it clear that she does in many respects have a richer mind, based on a richer culture than that of the Wentworths. Felix, for all of his artistic sensitivity and his inherited tradition of wide culture, is in certain senses a mere waster with a flippant disregard for many of the minor points of accepted morality. In this complexity of characterization and judgment, this larger comment on the mixture of the admirable and the regrettable in his characters, James carries on by means of the arts his more general thematic comment on the American intellectual atmosphere.

Through the European sensibility of Felix Young, the arts pervade *The Europeans,* and appear in a number of apparently unrelated images which are remarkably effective within the theme. The Wentworth family, for instance, is a great joy to Felix, and he applies to its members a typical metaphor: "He had never known anything more charming than the attention they paid to what he said. It was like a large

---

8. Ibid., p. 32.
9. Ibid., p. 97.
1. Ibid., p. 67.

sheet of clean, fine-grained drawing-paper, all ready to be washed over with effective splashes of water-color." [2] The image is effective in several ways. The comparison of the attention of the family, or of the family itself, to "clean, fine-grained drawing-paper" suggests the honest, simple, utilitarian attractiveness of the family, and also inevitably suggests an intellectual blankness, a "tabula rasa" which Felix is going to cover with "effective splashes of water-color." Yet water color is a difficult medium with which to work, and washes out almost as easily as it is put on; at best, it is difficult to keep the various colors from running together. Felix as an artist quite properly should use such images drawn from the arts, and he is reasonably consistent in using them. To take another example, there is attributed to him a description of the European women in his life: "He had known, fortunately, many virtuous gentlewomen, but it now appeared to him that in his relations with them (especially when they were unmarried) he had been looking at pictures under glass." [3] He continues and amplifies the image, but the reader must feel for himself the suggestive richness of "under glass" and "pictures." Now in America Felix sees the Wentworth ladies not as pictures through a glass, but finally face to face.

As the full effect of Felix begins to show in Gertrude Wentworth, it is not surprising to find her too beginning to think in tentative metaphors drawn from the arts, as though she had caught the habit from him. There is a feeling of imitation even in her emotional response when she sees a sunset as "the great picture of a New England sunset, painted in crimson and silver, . . . suspended from the zenith." [4] The image has an artificial, labored quality which suggests the strangeness of such a thought to this mind trained in the New England ethos, and yet suggests the new expansion of that mind. The labored quality is particularly apparent when Gertrude's image is compared with one of Felix' perfect metaphors, the full presentation of his sister, the Baroness: " 'She's even more of a European than I; here, you know, she's a picture out of her setting.' " [5] Eugenia has the beauty, the grace, the charm, the tradition of the ages, and yet also the artificialness, and the essentially imitative qualities of art. The description of this picture as out of its setting in America makes the full summation of the novel and the final comment on the theme of the American-European contrast.

2. Ibid., p. 83.
3. Ibid., p. 84.
4. Ibid., p. 108.
5. Ibid., p. 138.

4

The Theme of Moral Decision

BY the mid-eighties James had tired of the theme of the American-European contrast, and was looking for another center of interest: "For myself, at any rate, I am deadly weary of the whole 'international' state of mind—so that I *ache,* at times, with fatigue at the way it is constantly forced upon me as a sort of virtue or obligation."[1] Momentarily he even turned to parody of the subject in the pleasant little *The Reverberator*. But what he needed was a new theme or at least a new point of concentration which would offer an equally dramatic means of presenting the fascinating complexities of the human state. The international theme, with its implicit definition of the European and the American atmospheres, had demanded concentration on the background, the social and intellectual milieu, as an integral element of the character of the individual. Now James was to shift his emphasis, although by no means entirely, to the more nearly universal moral elements of the individual human being. This increasing interest, restricted yet more broadly and perhaps more meaningfully applicable, provides the thematic unity of his second group of novels: *The Portrait of a Lady* (1881), *The Princess Casamassima* (1886), *The Tragic Muse* (1890), and *The Spoils of Poynton* (1897).

Now that he was settled more or less permanently in England, the setting of the new novels provided no problem: "One thing only is clear, that henceforth I must do, or half do, England in fiction—as the place I see most today, and, in a sort of way, know best."[2] The new theme which he chose for this particular setting found its dramatization in the problem of the moral decision by the individual, an interest always latent in the earlier novels, and to become increasingly stronger through the rest of his work. The moral decision, however, is seldom a matter only of an ethical choice between right and wrong, but more often involves a choice between two ways of life, one offering some opportunity for a greater fulfillment of the possibilities of the human spirit, and the other offering eventual frustration and aridity. The moral interest of the four novels, incorporating the ethical but going beyond it to greater related values, is essentially a thoughtful and serious interest in the obligations and opportunities of the soul in this human life.

1. To William James, Oct. 29, 1888, in *Letters, 1,* 141.
2. To W. D. Howells, May 17, 1890, in *Letters, 1,* 166.

The theme is particularly embodied in each novel by the dramatic conflict or lack of conflict between this greater morality and esthetics. Eventually, as the novels themselves make clear, the conflict centers on the suggestive value, in James' particular definition almost the moral value, which is the mark of great art. It must be insisted immediately, however, that no such simplification is possible as that offered by one literary critic and apparently accepted by many: "The consciousness most sensitive to impressions is liable to be the most moral. So in James there is an equation between the esthetic and the moral sense, and the individual who most appreciates the beauty of a Renaissance painting is also the most moral." [3] James would have been horrified, and in fact several times in his novels attacked just such an easy assumption. The moral-esthetic relationship is far more complex, and its very complexity provides much of the interest of the novels. With the introduction of the moral-esthetic problem as one embodiment of a more general moral problem, the references to the visual arts in the novels have a particular interpretative value. For the arts, representing as they do one element of esthetic interest, are at the very center of the theme, and offer a valuable aid to understanding.

The Portrait of a Lady provides the earliest and quite possibly the best example, and like *The Spoils of Poynton* deserves consideration for its value as a novel as well as for its definition of the theme. *The Portrait of a Lady* too is particularly convenient in offering a transition between this second group of James' novels and the first, for it is in many respects a continuation and a fulfillment of the themes and techniques of the first group, in which it falls chronologically. The final sentences of James' later Preface to the novel stress the continued interest: "I had, within the few preceding years, come to live in London, and the 'international' light lay, in those days, to my sense, thick and rich upon the scene. It was the light in which so much of the picture hung." [4] The novel puts great emphasis, as do the earlier ones, on the general atmosphere of Europe, on the age and beauty and tradition not found in America. But even in this emphasis the novel does not entirely fit the pattern of the earlier group, for James' interest now lies not in the definition of the contrast but in a more direct fictional exploitation of its effect upon the sensibilities of the heroine, Isabel Archer. The earlier theme has become a means rather than an end in itself.

Although the age and tradition of Europe, the accumulated weight of the past, is assumed throughout the novel, its presence is still made abundantly clear. The novel opens with a scene on the lawn of the

---

3. John H. Raleigh, "Henry James: the Poetics of Empiricism," *PMLA*, 66 (Mar., 1951), 111.
4. Preface to *The Portrait of a Lady*, Collected Novels and Tales (New York, Charles Scribner's Sons, 1908), *3*, xxi.

Touchett house, a house with "a name and a history."[5] The reader is immediately plunged into the air of Europe, and throughout the novel is never allowed to forget the background and the tradition in which the story takes place. Characteristically for James, as various houses appear in the novel their representative value is carefully established. Mrs. Touchett's in Florence, "an historic building in a narrow street whose very name recalled the strife of mediaeval factions," holds "the spirit of the past . . . like a refugee from the outer world."[6] Osmond's ancient Florentine villa has an even stronger smell of the past, furnished as it is with "a variety of those faded hangings of damask and tapestry, those chests and cabinets of carved and time-polished oak, those primitive specimens of pictorial art in frames pedantically rusty, those perverse-looking relics of mediaeval brass and pottery, of which Italy has long been the not quite exhausted storehouse."[7] His Roman Palazzo Roccanera, frescoed and statued in the ancient manner, even seems to little Rosier a medieval dungeon "which smelt of historic deeds, of crime and craft and violence."[8] By the time Isabel reaches Italy she too begins to feel in such arts, for the reader as it were, the full meaning of the European scene. In a phrase that concentrates that meaning, James says, "The sense of the mighty human past was heavy upon her."[9]

The arts characterize Europe, but characterize even more vigorously, continuing the techniques of the earlier novels, the persons of the novel. Mr. Touchett, for instance, like Lord Warburton, is inseparable from his fine old house. When at the end of the novel Isabel returns to "her richly-constituted refuge,"[1] it is like a child coming home to an old friend. In contrast to these worthy, solid men, little Rosier, the American dilettante, appears as small and fragile as the *bibelots* which he collects. He is a lightweight, "a surface suggesting sprigged porcelain,"[2] a fragile *objet d'art* in this story of powerful forces in conflict, and at best he can only hope to escape unbroken. Yet in his small way, perhaps even because of it, he is capable of arousing pathos. In hopes of winning Pansy by satisfying her father's demands, he makes the supreme sacrifice:

> "It's very soon told," said Edward Rosier. "I have sold all my bibelots!"
>
> Isabel gave, instinctively, an exclamation of horror; it was as if he had told her he had had all his teeth drawn.

· · · ·

5. *The Portrait of a Lady* (Boston, Houghton, Mifflin & Co., 1882), p. 2.
6. Ibid., p. 215.
7. Ibid., p. 198.
8. Ibid., p. 319.
9. Ibid., p. 250.
1. Ibid., p. 491.
2. Ibid., p. 317.

> Rosier gave her a sharp look.
> "Do you mean that without my bibelots I am nothing? Do you mean that they were the best things about me? That's what they told me in Paris; oh, they were very frank about it. But they hadn't seen *her!*" [3]

The situation is both humorous and pathetic, for he is indeed nothing without his collection. With a magnificent gesture he has sold his own identity.

Completely unlike the enthusiastic little dilettante, two other Americans, Henrietta Stackpole and Caspar Goodwood, two ferocious critics in Europe, are free from any esthetic interest in the arts. As the American industrialist of granite-like strength and firm determination, doggedly pursuing his love, Caspar Goodwood represents all that Isabel has left behind, a life of honesty, of directness, of tangible purpose. He remains an outsider, a foreigner speaking another language in this exotic world of the arts, and has little in common with the Europeanized characters. In Henrietta, although she was like James Stackpole, himself once an art critic for an American journal, he finds the one other person who seems to speak—and write—his American language. She has come to Europe for the very practical purpose of sending back letters for the *Interviewer,* and is determined to allow nothing else to occupy her mind. But as she becomes increasingly drawn into Isabel's problems, her sense of firm American disapproval weakens. Unlike Caspar, the longer she stays in Italy the more interested she becomes in the "external," until at last a deepening appreciation of the esthetic adds to her character the necessary sympathetic element for true understanding of the scene about her. On one of her visits to Florence she even goes out of her way to see her favorite painting:

> Miss Stackpole may appear more ardent in her quest of artistic beauty than she has hitherto struck us as being, but she had after all her preferences and admirations. One of the latter was the little Correggio of the Tribune—the Virgin kneeling down before the sacred infant, who lies in a litter of straw, and clapping her hands to him while he delightedly laughs and crows. Henrietta had taken a great fancy to this intimate scene—she thought it the most beautiful picture in the world.[4]

Coming as the description does shortly before she announces her plans to marry, the "intimate scene" of the Correggio suggests a depth of feeling in Henrietta not hitherto suspected.

Similar examples are numerous. Pansy to little Rosier is always a

---

3. Ibid., pp. 462-3.
4. Ibid., p. 400.

tiny, exquisite work of art: "She was admirably finished—she was in excellent style. He thought of her in amorous meditation a good deal as he might have thought of a Dresden-china shepherdess. Miss Osmond, indeed, in the bloom of her juvenility, had a touch of the rococo, which Rosier, whose taste was predominantly for that manner, could not fail to appreciate." [5] Small, attractive, fashioned carefully by others, she becomes, in the midst of the crushing forces of the novel, simply an object of fragile beauty. In contrast, Mrs. Touchett, the Europeanized American, is a sinister force deliberately held in abeyance. Osmond's description of her is brilliant:

> "Oh, she's an old Florentine; I mean literally an old one; not a modern outsider. She is a contemporary of the Medici; she must have been present at the burning of Savonarola, and I am not sure she didn't throw a handful of chips into the flame. Her face is very much like some faces in the early pictures; little, dry, definite faces, that must have had a good deal of expression, but almost always the same one. Indeed, I can show you her portrait in a fresco of Ghirlandaio's." [6]

With due allowance for the mocking bitterness, the description does suggest certain potential traits of character inherent in her very inactivity.

For almost every character of the *The Portrait of a Lady* the visual arts provide a similar system of observation. But the interpretative value of the arts is even greater, for the arts themselves often provide a meaningful symbolism, leading the reader to the heart of the novel. Osmond's house, for instance, has an "imposing front" but "a somewhat incommunicative character," and the windows "seemed to be less to offer communication with the world than to defy the world to look in." [7] It looks "as if, once you were in, it would not be easy to get out." [8] Or again, a more detailed, an almost symbolic, presentation of Lord Warburton's position is offered in the scene where Isabel after refusing his hand finds him in the gallery of the Capitol, "standing before the lion of the collection, the statue of the Dying Gladiator." [9] A similar suggestiveness close to the symbolic may be seen even in the very opening of the novel where Mr. Touchett sits at ease drinking his tea: "The old man had his cup in his hand; it was an unusually large cup, of a different pattern from the rest of the set, and painted in brilliant colours. He disposed of its contents with much circumspection, holding it for a long time close to his chin, with his face turned to the

---

5. Ibid., p. 313.
6. Ibid., p. 226.
7. Ibid., pp. 197-8.
8. Ibid., p. 221.
9. Ibid., p. 262.

house." [1] The cup as a symbol for life is traditional—James had used it before in the little statue of the water drinker in *Roderick Hudson* —and this cup has a high suggestiveness.

With minor characters the subject of such care, it is to be expected that the arts offer a similar interpretation, of greater scope and detail, of the major characters as well. With a few quick strokes young Rosier stands alive as the likeable young dilettante. It is almost the method of caricature, and the eternal bibelots suggest the method of Dickens, the association of each character with one particular thing or with one particular phrase. In many respects Gilbert Osmond, a major character of the novel, is portrayed in the same manner, although there is more, much more, to him. He too is introduced as an inspired dilettante, and never loses that particular character. When first seen in the novel he is showing off his latest water color, and when last seen he is copying a drawing of an antique coin. Within such a frame his life is carefully painted.

Osmond surrounds himself with beautiful objects; his accumulation is so great that it is even oppressive. Madame Merle, whose taste at least can be trusted, leaves no doubt of the perfection of his choice: "She looked about the room—at the old cabinets, the pictures, the tapestries, the surfaces of faded silk. 'Your rooms, at least, are perfect,' she went on. 'I am struck with that afresh, whenever I come back; I know none better anywhere. You understand this sort of thing as no one else does.'" [2] His choice is not surprising, for as "student of the exquisite," [3] he is faultless. It is impossible not to think of him in connection with art; he lives surrounded by it, he lives in it and for it. Like young Rosier, his taste and his collections are his character. The arts are so much a part of Gilbert Osmond that at times he is even described in terms of them. His life and thought, "the mansion of his own habitation," are as forbidding as his house itself: "It was the house of darkness, the house of dumbness, the house of suffocation. Osmond's beautiful mind gave it neither light nor air; Osmond's beautiful mind, indeed, seemed to peep down from a small high window and mock at her." [4] Madame Merle early likens him to a collection of snuffboxes,[5] and even Isabel at first acquaintance thinks him "as fine as one of the drawings in the long gallery above the bridge, at the Uffizi." [6] Even his beard is "cut in the manner of the portraits of the sixteenth century." [7]

1. Ibid., pp. 1–2.
2. Ibid., p. 211.
3. Ibid., p. 239.
4. Ibid., p. 375.
5. Ibid., p. 172.
6. Ibid., p. 216.
7. Ibid., p. 199.

THE THEME OF MORAL DECISION

Despite this exquisite taste and this passion for beauty, his esthetic judgment is seen increasingly clearly as something cold and ugly and evil. It is here that James begins to define what is to be the central theme of his second group of novels. For to Osmond moral judgment is merely a matter of esthetics, the position, ironically enough, into which some critics have even tried to force Henry James himself.[8] But as James makes clear, judgment on the purely esthetic level is the judgment of selfishness and egotism, a refusal of the accepted codes of behavior in favor of a private code based on personal taste. The repellent egotism of such a code is dramatically apparent in Osmond's continual attempt to live only by taste and by appreciation of form, form of the visual and of the social and traditional. " 'He has a great dread of vulgarity; that's his special line; he hasn't any other that I know of,' "[9] says Ralph Touchett. Osmond's possessions are chosen for their beauty, and his family is as much a part of his possessions as any picture or tapestry. His daughter is just another ornament to him, a piece not to be matched,[1] "a precious work of art,"[2] and he can even feel an "aesthetic relish of Pansy's innocence."[3] Isabel he has intended as his greatest ornament, "a young lady who had qualified herself to figure in his collection of choice objects,"[4] an extension of his own ego. His taste would be hers, and he could enjoy her both as a possession and as a projection of himself. She will offer a valuable new display: "His egotism, if egotism it was, had never taken the crude form of wishing for a dull wife; this lady's intelligence was to be a silver plate, not an earthen one —a plate that he might heap up with ripe fruits, to which it would give a decorative value, so that conversation might become a sort of perpetual dessert. He found the silvery quality in perfection in Isabel; he could tap her imagination with his knuckle and make it ring."[5]

In a moment of dramatic irony, Isabel says in all sincerity, after hearing Osmond describe his life in Italy, " 'That's a very pleasant life, . . . to renounce everything but Correggio!' "[6] It is only after it is too late that she sees, like the wife of Mark Ambient in *The Author of Beltraffio*, the deadening evil of a life devoted to the esthetic and nothing more. By this insistence on the importance of moral sensitivity to esthetics, as to any part of life, *The Portrait of a Lady* takes its place in the second group of James' novels. For it is the emphasis not on the importance of taste to life but on the importance of human morality to

8. Cf. Stuart P. Sherman, "The Aesthetic Idealism of Henry James," in *On Contemporary Literature* (New York, Henry Holt & Co., 1917), p. 236.
9. *Portrait of a Lady*, p. 218.
1. Ibid., p. 321.
2. Ibid., p. 467.
3. Ibid., p. 309.
4. Ibid., p. 264.
5. Ibid., p. 307.
6. Ibid., p. 232.

taste that shows the central meaning of the novel. Osmond's most horrible thought, horrible because it describes the ideal which he follows literally, is that " 'one ought to make one's life a work of art.' " [7] It is James' repulsion from such a life that gives the novel so much of its strength. Taste, appreciation, love of the beautiful are not enough; a true morality, a feeling for the life of others, is the necessary adjunct of taste, and without it only egotism, sterility, and evil can follow. As the full ugliness of Gilbert Osmond's life becomes apparent, Ralph Touchett's bitter condemnation takes on added strength: " 'He is the incarnation of taste. . . . He judges and measures, approves and condemns, altogether by that.' " [8]

Madame Merle too has impeccable taste. Like Osmond's, her house is beautifully furnished, and like him she has great knowledge of art. Her answer to Isabel's denial of interest in the house of any possible lover might have come from Osmond himself: " 'That is very crude of you. When you have lived as long as I, you will see that every human being has his shell, and that you must take the shell into account. By the shell I mean the whole envelope of circumstances. There is no such thing as an isolated man or woman; we are each of us made up of a cluster of appurtenances,' " [9] Yet Madame Merle too is morally imperfect. Her evil arises not from too great a concern for her own values, however, but too great a concern for the values of others: "If for Isabel she had a fault, it was . . . that her nature had been too much overlaid by custom and her angles too much smoothed. She had become too flexible, too supple; she was too finished, too civilised. She was, in a word, too perfectly the social animal that man and woman are supposed to have been intended to be." [1] She is capable of moral wrong, she can hide the guilt of Pansy's birth, and she can lead Isabel to a tragic marriage, but it is a wrong demanded by the society into which she fits so smoothly. In the tradition of James' earlier novels she is a part of Europe, and cannot be judged by American standards: " 'Ah, my dear *je viens de loin;* I belong to the old world.' " [2] Her esthetic taste is not, like Osmond's, the cause of her sorrow and her guilt, but no more can it lessen or excuse them.

The esthetic and the social forces in Madame Merle's life both appear in two small but admirable examples of James' related symbolism of the arts. In the first she makes the meaning obvious. Isabel had been saying that so few people have ever felt anything deeply, and Madame Merle replies:

7. Ibid., p. 269.
8. Ibid., p. 302.
9. Ibid., p. 175.
1. Ibid., p. 167.
2. Ibid., p. 170.

"It's very true; there are more iron pots, I think, than porcelain ones. But you may depend upon it that everyone has something; even the hardest iron pots have a little bruise, a little hole, somewhere. I flatter myself that I am rather stout porcelain; but if I must tell you the truth I have been chipped and cracked! I do very well for service yet, because I have been cleverly mended; and I try to remain in the cupboard—the quiet, dusky cupboard, where there is an odour of stale spices—as much as I can. But when I have to come out, and into a strong light, then, my dear, I am a horror!" [3]

This image of the moral flaw as a crack in porcelain, suggestive of *The Golden Bowl* yet to come, appears again later in the novel. There as Madame Merle and Osmond talk together, and she has reached to some degree a point of recognition of her own guilt, Osmond looks over her rare porcelain, and picks up a small cup. On being warned to take care, he answers dryly that it already has a crack. "After he had left her, Madame Merle went and lifted from the mantel-shelf the attenuated coffee-cup in which he had mentioned the existence of a crack; but she looked at it rather abstractedly. 'Have I been so vile all for nothing?' she murmured to herself." [4] The two examples, even coming as they do many pages apart, provide mutual reinforcement, and contribute with successful indirection to the painstaking characterization of the novel.

All the characters are individually portrayed, but *The Portrait of a Lady* is primarily the story of Isabel Archer, the sensitive young American confronted with Europe for the first time. Life in America had been for her but a preparation for Europe, and even her house there suggests the qualities of this preliminary period: comfortable enough, handsome enough, and even with traditions of its own. But, as Mrs. Touchett says, " 'In Florence we should call it a very bad house.' " [5] Fittingly, the room in which Isabel is first found by Mrs. Touchett is just off the library: "She had never opened the bolted door nor removed the green paper (renewed by other hands) from its side-lights; she had never assured herself that the vulgar street lay beyond it." [6] Taken suddenly from such a limited room to the full splendor of Gardencourt, Isabel discovers her immense passion for experience, a reminder that this novel continues and fulfills the thematic pattern established by the earlier novels. She is keen, she is perceptive, and she has a remarkably active imagination. Her self-confidence is perhaps a major flaw, but it is an admirable one which drives her into the full experience

3. Ibid., p. 168.
4. Ibid., p. 461.
5. Ibid., p. 21.
6. Ibid., p. 19.

of life. A highly responsive innocence is prepared to absorb Europe, but in reality is prepared only to be absorbed by Europe.

Innocent though she may be, her taste in the arts is sufficiently developed to allow her to mingle with this group of Europeans and Europeanized Americans, so sensitive to esthetic values, without inferiority. As Ralph Touchett soon discovers, "She was evidently a judge; she had a natural taste; he was struck with that." [7] Just as important as her taste, her interest in the arts is great:

> She went to the galleries and palaces; she looked at the pictures and statues which had hitherto been great names to her, and exchanged for a knowledge which was sometimes a limitation a presentiment which proved usually to have been a blank. She performed all those acts of mental prostration in which, on a first visit to Italy, youth and enthusiasm so freely indulge; she felt her heart beat in the presence of immortal genius, and knew the sweetness of rising tears in eyes to which faded fresco and darkened marble grew dim.[8]

Her response to art is emotional and immediate. She is no ordinary tourist, and on her first visit to St. Peter's, "her conception of greatness received an extension." [9] But this love of art and desire for knowledge is her undoing, for it leads her into marriage with Gilbert Osmond, the learned dilettante.

By the time Isabel finds for herself that Osmond is nothing more than the " 'sterile dilettante' " [1] which Ralph Touchett knows him to be, it is too late, and she has devoted her life to a teacher who has nothing to offer but knowledge. She finds too late that "to renounce everything but Correggio" is a life not of fulfillment but of sterility. The true knowledge of art which she so desires comes only when she knows instinctively and deeply that art alone is not enough, that a feeling for morality, for life, for the human element is even more important. The recognition of this truth appears in her growing feeling for Rome, the sights and objects of which no longer evoke mere esthetic pleasure, but a full sympathy with the human condition:

> She had long before this taken old Rome into her confidence, for in a world of ruins the ruin of her happiness seemed a less unnatural catastrophe. She rested her weariness upon things that had crumbled for centuries and yet still were upright; she dropped her secret sadness into the silence of lonely places, where its very modern quality detached itself and grew objective, so that as she sat in

---

7. Ibid., p. 38.
8. Ibid., p. 215.
9. Ibid., p. 257.
1. Ibid., p. 303.

a sun-warmed angle on a winter's day, or stood in a mouldy church to which no one came, she could almost smile at it and think of its smallness. Small it was, in the large Roman record, and her haunting sense of the continuity of the human lot easily carried her from the less to the greater.[2]

Isabel does not make a religion of the arts as Osmond has done, but rather finds something closely approaching the religious inherent in the arts and suggested by them.

Gilbert Osmond's view of Isabel as only a superior work of art is frightening in its portrayal of his own mind, but within the imagery of the novel it has a certain validity. For Isabel does have the human value of a great work of art. Ralph Touchett, probably the keenest mind in the novel, feels the comparison immediately:

> "A character like that," he said to himself, "is the finest thing in nature. It is finer than the finest work of art—than a Greek bas-relief, than a great Titian, than a Gothic cathedral."
>
> . . . .
>
> "Suddenly I receive a Titian, by the post, to hang on my wall—a Greek bas-relief to stick over my chimney-piece. The key of a beautiful edifice is thrust into my hand, and I am told to walk in and admire." [3]

Others soon echo his thoughts as well as his admiration. Mrs. Touchett compares her, in one of Isabel's solemn moods, to a Cimabue Madonna,[4] and young Rosier sees her, "framed in the gilded doorway, . . . as the picture of a gracious lady." [5] The title then, *The Portrait of a Lady,* is more fitting than might at first appear. For not only is the novel itself, by a traditional metaphor, a portrait, but the subject of that portrait is herself a work of art, a portrait, as it were, of the young girl eager to find and catch the finer life but trapped in that very desire by the evil forces which use her possibilities for their own petty ends.

As Isabel enters further into the tragedy of her marriage to Gilbert Osmond she attempts to hide her suffering, to disguise the natural portrait by art: "If she wore a mask, it completely covered her face. There was something fixed and mechanical in the serenity painted upon it; this was not an expression, Ralph said—it was a representation." [6] Isabel is forcing herself into an artificial pose, a false portrait. Her desire is no longer to meet the full shock of life—that does not recur until her triumphal return to her husband to see the misery through

2. Ibid., p. 454.
3. Ibid., pp. 52–3.
4. Ibid., p. 183.
5. Ibid., p. 321.
6. Ibid., p. 343.

as best she can—but rather to hide from life as much as possible. "It seemed to her an act of devotion to conceal her misery from him. She concealed it elaborately; in their talk she was perpetually hanging out curtains and arranging screens." [7] The screen she erects, however, is not so much to protect herself as to save others from pain. The contrast with Osmond is carefully drawn, for his represents hypocrisy, not generosity, and he attempts disguise to hide his own evil motives. With rasping irony Isabel says, upon hearing his house praised, " 'He has a genius for upholstery,' " [8] and the phrase neatly covers both his taste and his hypocrisy. As the full realization of Osmond's aridity and evil comes to Isabel, and she begins to screen the sight of her pain from her friends, she finds herself equally screened in by his pervading egotistic power. "When Isabel saw this rigid system closing about her, draped though it was in pictured tapestries, that sense of darkness and suffocation . . . took possession of her; she seemed to be shut up with an odour of mould and decay." [9] About this ghastly situation she in turn again erects her own series of screens. The effect of the imagery is that of a formal maze, one screen within another, and this constant, intricate, and involuted attempt to disguise, to screen, to mask represents the lowest point of Isabel in the novel. For she was meant to be original, to be natural, to be the full portrait of confident, zestful life. Any attempt to turn the portrait to the wall is unnatural and disturbing.

Ralph Touchett, the one character who makes a success of life, prefers the full and original portrait. It is even he, of all the characters of the novel, who compares her most objectively to a work of art, "a Titian, a Greek bas-relief, a beautiful edifice." Yet his description does not imply a limited esthetic view, as it does for Osmond, but rather a full response to the greater beauty of the human being. The distinction may be felt more clearly, perhaps, in such a short story as *The Beldonald Holbein,* where Mrs. Brash is consistently discussed by the narrator as "a Holbein," not simply in esthetic response to her physical likeness to a Holbein, but in response to the beauty of character reflected in her face. Similarly, Ralph Touchett began his comparison with a careful distinction between art and nature: Isabel is like a work of art, but is even finer, for she is a part of nature. The distinction is fitting, for of the various relations to the arts shown in the novel, his alone is consistently sane and admirable. And the most admirable quality of this relation is his insistence on the greater importance of life than art.

Ralph does not scorn the esthetic, as do Henrietta Stackpole and Caspar Goodwood, but neither does he give it the worship of a Gilbert Osmond. "Ralph had something of . . . this appearance of thinking

---

7. Ibid., p. 380.
8. Ibid., p. 337.
9. Ibid., p. 377.

that life was a matter of connoisseurship; but in Ralph it was an anomaly, a kind of humorous excrescence, whereas in Mr. Osmond it was the key-note, and everything was in harmony with it." [1] His gallery at Gardencourt is a good one; most of the pictures he chose himself. He is obviously proud of it, and like so many of James' more sensitive characters he likes to talk and think there. But its relative importance to life, to the real thing, is made clear when he first shows Isabel the pictures. "He found himself pausing in the middle of the gallery and bending his eyes much less upon the pictures than on her figure. He lost nothing, in truth, by these wandering glances; for she was better worth looking at than most works of art." [2] This humanistic attitude (the element of sensuousness does not lessen it), as contrasted with the esthetic or the practical attitudes of the other Europeanized Americans in the novel, defines his essentially moral view of life, and increases his bond of natural sympathy with Isabel.

The contrast of Ralph's physical weakness and humanistic strength is made the more thematically significant by what at first appears a passing reference to the arts. Ralph is showing Henrietta Stackpole the gallery. As usual with him, he introduces the subject in casually humorous fashion:

> "Ah," said Ralph, "I am the idlest man living."
> Miss Stackpole turned her gaze to the Constable again, and Ralph bespoke her attention for a small Watteau hanging near it, which represented a gentleman in a pink doublet and hose and a ruff, leaning against the pedestal of the statue of a nymph in a garden, and playing the guitar to two ladies seated on the grass.
> "That's my ideal of a regular occupation," he said.[3]

At the moment, so early in the novel, his idea does little more than shock Henrietta and suggest a very normal yearning for a pleasant pastoral life. But much later in the novel Isabel finds Ralph one warm morning in Mrs. Touchett's Italian garden, "sitting there in the clear gloom, at the base of a statue of Terpsichore—a dancing nymph with taper fingers and inflated draperies, in the manner of Bernini." [4] The immediate conjunction of the consumptive Ralph and the muse of dancing is itself an ironic touch, perhaps suggesting his early remark that in the anteroom of his mind he always keeps a band of music because " 'it makes the world think that dancing is going on within.' " [5] But the suggestiveness of the visual image, in relation to the small Watteau at Gardencourt, is enormous. Ralph, even in his dying state, likes to sit

1. Ibid., p. 229.
2. Ibid., p. 38.
3. Ibid., pp. 75–6.
4. Ibid., p. 298.
5. Ibid., p. 50.

at the feet of the dancing muse and play while others dance. He had earlier told his father, when requesting a legacy for Isabel, that he would derive great amusement from watching her progress through life. Now he furnishes the music while she dances, although the amusement, in the face of her tragic life, is hardly so pleasant as he had anticipated. Yet he is still in love with her in a way that goes beyond passion. For just as his love of art is merged with a moral grasp of life, so his love of Isabel is merged with a love of life itself. He makes her a part of his very life; she is his activity and his dance. When her first rapturous zeal for living is crushed, he dies with it. But the nymph "in the manner of Bernini," bringing together life and art into one moral whole, continues to stand erect and beautiful.

Just as great art could not for Ralph, as for James himself, be divorced from an evocation of some more universal insight, so too in all these novels of James' middle life an esthetic sensitivity cannot or must not be divorced from a sensitivity to the greater truths and the greater promises of human life. Isabel Archer and Ralph Touchett find the two sensibilities synonymous. Hyacinth Robinson in *The Princess Casamassima* and Nick Dormer in *The Tragic Muse* eventually make the same discovery. For Hyacinth, however, as for Isabel Archer, the discovery is a gradual one. *The Princess Casamassima* begins with the young, sensitive Hyacinth, convinced of vague aristocratic birth, trapped in a dull life of poverty and banality. An early concern with anarchism is simply his first gesture toward some better life for himself and for others. But as he matures it becomes increasingly apparent that the better life which he so desires is the life of means and beauty, the life represented in his own observation and experience by the arts. With that discovery, however, he makes the parallel discovery that the anarchism which he had espoused is not only futile but a danger to the very life which he has defined for his wishes. The double discovery is too late, however, and trapped in his own confusions, deeply disappointed by the casual betrayals and shallow morality of the friends around him, he finds no solution but to turn the pistol, supposedly devoted to the anarchic cause, against his own head. He cannot live in the poor, dull, ugly, working world of Lomax Place, and he cannot reach permanently the beautiful world of Paris or the country house, the life represented by the arts.

Lomax Place, Hyacinth's shabby childhood home so reminiscent of the novels of Dickens, is not so much lacking in the arts as lacking in taste. The showroom of the house, for instance, in addition to the implements of the dressmaking craft which supports it, contains "the everlasting sofa . . . covered with a light, shrunken shroud of a strange yellow stuff, the tinge of which revealed years of washing, and surmounted by a coloured print of Rebekah at the Well, balancing, in the opposite quarter, with a portrait of the Empress of the French, taken from an illustrated newspaper and framed and glazed in the manner of 1853." [6] Then too, there is "the chimney-piece, on which a design, partly architectural, partly botanical, executed in the hair of Miss Pynsent's parents, was flanked by a pair of vases, under glass, containing muslin flowers." [7] If the description is realistic, with even a touch of humor, the power of definition in the brooding mind of Hyacinth is no less valid. He begins to feel the definition on his return to Lomax Place after his first visit to the country house of the Italian Princess, and the contrast is expressed in terms of the arts:

> The picture was the same, and all its horrid elements, wearing a kind of greasy gloss in the impure air of Lomax Place, made, through the mean window-panes, a dismal *chiaroscuro*—showed, in their polished misery, the friction of his own little life; but the eyes with which he looked at it had new terms of comparison. He had known the place was hideous and sordid, but its aspect to-day was pitiful to the verge of the sickening; he couldn't believe that for years together he had accepted and even, a little, revered it.[8]

From the moment of this repelling impression he can never again accept Lomax Place, and can only dream of another world.

As his observation and experience grow, Hyacinth quickly learns to discriminate between the two worlds by the esthetic quality of their physical appearance. The gauge is not his alone, of course, for the Princess herself, in idle boredom sampling the life of genteel poverty, had first to arrive at the same conclusion: "It was plainly her theory that the right way to acquaint one's self with the sensations of the wretched was to suffer the anguish of exasperated taste." [9] But it is not until Hyacinth visits the continent and discovers an ecstatic appreciation of Paris and Venice that the gauge becomes for him emotionally undeniable. Seen from these living museums, his old life in London, the life of all the masses for whom he had once felt so strongly, carries in retrospect the full shock of ugliness:

> Our young man took almost the same sort of satisfaction in the Louvre as if he had erected it; he haunted the museum during all the first days, couldn't look enough at certain pictures, nor sufficiently admire the high polish of the great floors in which the golden, frescoed ceilings repeated themselves. All Paris struck him as tremendously artistic and decorative; he felt as if hitherto he

---

6. *The Princess Casamassima* (3 vols. London and New York, Macmillan & Co., 1886), *1*, 54.
7. Ibid., *1*, 58.
8. Ibid., *2*, 177.
9. Ibid., *3*, 7–8.

> had lived in a dusky, frowsy, Philistine world, in which the taste was the taste of Little Peddlington and the idea of beautiful arrangement had never had an influence.[1]

The resulting change in political and social thought, always latent in him, is seen immediately in his somewhat improbable letter from Venice:

> "The monuments and treasures of art, the great palaces and properties, the conquests of learning and taste, the general fabric of civilisation as we know it, based, if you will, upon all the despotisms, the cruelties, the exclusions, the monopolies and the rapacities of the past, but thanks to which, all the same, the world is less impracticable and life more tolerable—our friend Hoffendahl [the Anarchist leader] seems to me to hold them too cheap and to wish to substitute for them something in which I can't somehow believe as I do in things with which the aspirations and the tears of generations have been mixed." [2]

In the light of James' own beliefs, one is reminded of Lionel Trilling's argument [3] that Hyacinth is to a great extent a representative of James' own mind.

After the treasures of the continent, the social problem for Hyacinth is no longer that of anarchism and destruction, or even of socialism and amelioration. The real possibilities of life, the finer existence, lie in that world represented by taste, and based, unfortunately for social and political thought, upon wealth and leisure. Upon his return to London, then, Hyacinth is only in conscience on the side of the masses: "He saw the immeasurable misery of the people, and yet he saw all that had been, as it were, rescued and redeemed from it: the treasures, the felicities, the splendours, the successes, of the world." [4] The conflict in his mind has resolved itself to that of esthetics or economics, the finer life of the spirit or the finer life of the body, and the young Hyacinth, without learning or experience, surrounded by treachery and indifference, can only resolve the conflict with a bullet.

Ironically enough, his true calling as a bookbinder, a skilled and perceptive artist-craftsman, might have been his salvation. As an old friend says of his binding, too late, " 'You have a manner, like a master. With such a talent, such a taste, your future leaves nothing to be desired. You will make a fortune and become a great celebrity.' " [5] It is true that his

---

1. Ibid., *2*, 209.
2. Ibid., *2*, 229–230.
3. Lionel Trilling, "The Princess Casamassima," in *The Liberal Imagination* (New York, Viking Press, 1950), pp. 58–92.
4. *Casamassima*, *3*, 40.
5. Ibid., *3*, 201.

taste, leading him to his moral-esthetic discovery, has been admirable from the beginning. At one point the Princess expresses her surprise at this: " 'You come out of the hole you have described to me, and yet you might have stayed in country-houses all your life.' " [6] The modern reader is perhaps even more surprised, accustomed as he is to judge by the standards of realism. But such judgment is unfair to *The Princess Casamassima,* for there the stress is put not on the real but on the dream, not on the world as it is but on the world as it should be. The fable of the novel is the private one Hyacinth discovers for himself: "His last week at Medley [the country house] . . . had already become a kind of fable, the echo of a song; he could read it over like a story, gaze at it as he would have gazed at some exquisite picture." [7] Like Isabel Archer, he finds that although the relationship of esthetics to the greater morality, the greater potentialities of life, is no simple one, yet for him it is at the very center and basis of life itself.

So too for Nick Dormer of *The Tragic Muse,* the novel which James wrote out of a long considered interest: "To 'do something about art' —art, that is, as a human complication and a social stumbling-block— must have been for me early a good deal of a nursed intention, the conflict between art and 'the world' striking me thus betimes as one of the half-dozen great primary motives." [8] He might have said the same of any one of the novels in this great central group, accurately defining the common theme of all. It is particularly fitting for *The Tragic Muse,* however, where the conflict of art and the world is so explicitly defined, and the various ramifications of the problem so carefully and directly explored, that F. W. Dupee can speak of "the rational, four-square, patiently documented, day-light world of *The Tragic Muse,* in which the theme of art versus politics is explored with almost the consistency of a formal debate." [9] James, no longer skirting about the central theme, attacks it in this novel directly and with full vigor.

Half the novel is given to the struggle of Nick Dormer to win the muse of painting and to overcome his materially successful life, represented in part by Mrs. Dallow, the woman whom he loves but who represents all the forces opposed to his desire for a life devoted to art. The other half of the novel is given to the related story of Miriam Rooth, the brilliant, artful, selfish, young actress who in a similar manner sacrifices to her particular art her lover and the possibilities of the materially successful life so desired by her mother. Through both plots runs the continual conversation of Gabriel Nash, in so many ways a

---

6. Ibid., *2,* 149.
7. Ibid., *2,* 211.
8. Preface to *The Tragic Muse,* Collected Novels and Tales (New York, Charles Scribner's Sons, 1908), *7,* v.
9. F. W. Dupee, *Henry James,* American Men of Letters Series ([New York], William Sloane Associates, 1951), p. 162.

caricature of the *fin de siècle* esthete, whose life—or at least whose talk—is devoted only to the appreciation of the beautiful. In his role as an effete modern chorus he makes the central issues explicit, and serves beautifully to point the moral and adorn the tale.

Two such distinct plots, parallel though they are in many respects, presented to James a considerable problem of form and unity. The Preface shows his awareness of the problem when, after mentioning his horror of two pictures in one, he says, "It was a fact, apparently, that one *had* on occasion seen two pictures in one; were there not for instance certain sublime Tintorettos at Venice, a measureless Crucifixion in especial, which showed without loss of authority half a dozen actions separately taking place? Yes, that might be, but there had surely been nevertheless a mighty pictorial fusion, so that the virtue of composition had somehow thereby come all mysteriously to its own." [1] He finally decides that the key to the "pictorial fusion" of *The Tragic Muse* is the figure of Miriam Rooth, central to both plots and the unifying "tone." Certainly her relations with the various characters, within the action of the story itself, are apparent on first reading, and produce an interlocking movement of story, the consistent "tone" of which he speaks. In discussing this compositional function of Miriam, however, he unknowingly suggests still another means of unification. For he says that although he thought of Miriam as symbolic and functional, "her image had seemed susceptible of a livelier and 'prettier' concretion." [2] To take his expression literally for a moment, Miriam is indeed susceptible of a prettier "concretion," for in the novel her portrait is twice painted by Nick Dormer. And these portraits form in themselves another related center of composition.

The portraits are, of course, extensions of the image, carefully evoked through the novel, of Miriam herself as a work of art. "He could paint Miriam, day after day, without any agitating blur of vision; in fact the more he saw of her the clearer grew the atmosphere through which she blazed, the more her richness became one with that of the flowering picture." [3] Like the portrait in the short story *The Liar* or in *The Story of a Masterpiece,* the very paintings are an aid to clarity of vision and insight. But the portraits also represent at once Miriam and the fulfillment of the ambitions of Nick. From the first time Nick meets Miriam he wants to paint her, and the wish sums up his desire for the life of art. After abandoning the life of material promise, hers is the first portrait he paints, and so in a concrete way it represents the achievement of his desire. Their function is equally apparent in the fact that the final decision of Mrs. Dallow to break her engagement to Nick comes as the

1. Preface to *Tragic Muse,* p. ix.
2. Ibid., p. xvi.
3. *The Tragic Muse* (2 vols. Boston and New York, Houghton, Mifflin & Co., 1890), *2,* 811.

result of finding Nick in the act of painting Miriam. For her that portrait represents all the lost political and social hopes for Nick, the symbol of his refusal to enter the powerful and fashionable world which she so wants for them both.

The portraits, like the central portrait of *The Tone of Time,* form an axle about which the varied events of the novel revolve, a central point at which all meet. But more important to the central theme, the portraits also serve to stress certain characteristics of Nick himself. If they represent his choice of the potentialities of a life in which art is more important than money or position, in the last chapters of the novel they also suggest an ironic tone not previously noticed. For it is only there that Nick begins to suspect his own ability, all too easily gained, which has been so impressive in the portraits. "That they were wonderfully clever was just the detestable thing in them, so active had that cleverness been in making them seem better than they were." [4] Looking at them in moments of depression, he begins to despair of the future results of this cleverness: "Cheap and easy results would dangle before him, little amateurish conspicuities, helped by his history, at exhibitions." [5] Such fears might seem an admirable self-knowledge and a guard against the future, but portents of just such a future are thick at the end of the novel. Gabriel Nash has warned Nick that Mrs. Dallow will win him back by asking him to paint her portrait, and at the very end of the story, set in the future, just such a portrait is mentioned. Whether it is Nick or Mrs. Dallow who has by that time "come around" is left in doubt, but suspicions of Nick are inevitable.

There is little serious irony in *The Tragic Muse,* however, for behind any literary technique the novel is essentially a direct attempt to present the importance of art in the life of man. Gabriel Nash may be a comic figure, but he does express the central theme of the novel: "Gabriel maintained precisely that there were more ideas, more of those that man lived by, in a single room of the National Gallery than in all the statutes of Parliament." [6] (The possible pun on "statutes" is characteristic.) Again and again in the novel one feels the emotional intensity of James' thematic preoccupation with the close relationship of art to life. The possibility of serious ironic intention is destroyed by one passage alone in which James lyrically states his faith, illustrated so profusely by all of his novels, in the significance of great art to human life and human history. Nick Dormer is thinking of the great masterpieces of art inherited from the past:

> These were the things that were the most inspiring, in the sense that they were the things that, while generations, while worlds had

4. Ibid., *2,* 802.
5. Ibid., *2,* 803.
6. Ibid., *2,* 694.

come and gone, seemed most to survive and testify. As he stood before them sometimes the perfection of their survival struck him as the supreme eloquence, the reason that included all others, thanks to the language of art, the richest and most universal. Empires and systems and conquests had rolled over the globe and every kind of greatness had risen and passed away, but the beauty of the great pictures had known nothing of death or change, and the ages had only sweetened their freshness. The same faces, the same figures looked out at different centuries, knowing a deal the century didn't, and when they joined hands they made the indestructible thread on which the pearls of history were strung.[7]

In this emotional intensity, rather than in the simple interest shown in the stage, is to be found the important autobiographical element of the novel.

An honest belief in the human value of art makes *The Tragic Muse* more than a story; like *The Princess Casamassima,* it is a myth, an allegory of the struggle of the higher values of man against his pragmatic society. In a greater sense, Gabriel Nash's description of great portraiture is not irrelevant to *The Tragic Muse* itself: "It offered a double vision, the strongest dose of life that art could give, the strongest dose of art that life could give."[8] Life and art are inseparable, and together create a higher morality to which man must conform if he is to find his greatest potentialities. But the choice is not easy, and often demands a high price. For Nick Dormer it costs all peace of mind; for Isabel Archer it costs a life of suffering with the man she loaths; for Hyacinth Robinson it costs his very life; and for Fleda Vetch of *The Spoils of Poynton* it costs the man she loves and ironically even a great collection of art.

In *The Spoils of Poynton* the immediate struggle is between the widowed Mrs. Gereth and the fiancée of her son for possession of the beautiful furnishings of Poynton, the Gereth house, willed by Mr. Gereth entirely to his son. Caught in this struggle is Fleda Vetch, a sensitive and attractive young girl, one of James' "free natures," who falls in love with Owen Gereth and finds herself trapped by the moral problems involved. As a final denouement, Fleda gives up Owen to Mona Brigstock, his grasping fiancée, and sees Poynton and all its "spoils," the original source of contention, burnt to the ground. Fleda Vetch provides the filtering intelligence through which events are seen, and so provides, in function somewhat like Miriam Rooth, one source of unity for the tightly constructed novel. But James, discussing the problems of organization and emphasis, says in the Preface that "the

7. Ibid., 2, 827–8.
8. Ibid., 2, 461.

felt beauty and value of . . . the Things"⁹ should have been the real center, and adds:

> Yes, it is a story of cabinets and chairs and tables; they formed the bone of contention, but what would merely "become" of them, magnificently passive, seemed to represent a comparatively vulgar issue. The passions, the faculties, the forces their beauty would, like that of antique Helen of Troy, set in motion, was what, as a painter, one had really wanted of them, was the power in them that one had from the first appreciated. Emphatically, by that truth, there would have to be moral developments.¹

Between the passions of selfishness and self-sacrifice, love of possessions and love of beauty, the moral developments are extended. Again the complex relationship between esthetics and a higher morality, here touching even more directly a problem in ethics, defines and illustrates the theme which the novel bears in common with those others of the central group.

In keeping with the theme, the four principal persons of the novel are differentiated by their relation to the arts. Mrs. Gereth in particular exists almost comically in such a relationship; her esthetic taste is her character, and Poynton in its exquisite unity of tone and effect, its immediate example of the highest in the arts, is only an extension of her taste. "The mind's eye could see Mrs. Gereth, indeed, only in her thick, colored air; it took all the light of her treasures to make her concrete and distinct." ² Owen, her bumbling, helpless, dense and likable son, has no such feeling for Poynton beyond a vague sense of pleasure and pride. If the arts of Poynton are "furniture" to him—"the word, on his lips, had somehow, for Fleda, the sound of washing-stands and copious bedding" ³—it is apparent that for Mona Brigstock, his fiancée, they are simply the "spoils" to which she is entitled. " 'She thinks they're all right,' " ⁴ is the best Owen can say of her. But the Brigstocks' country house, Waterbath, is enough to convict the whole family: "They had gone wildly astray over carpets and curtains; they had an infallible instinct for disaster, and were so cruelly doom-ridden that it rendered them almost tragic." ⁵ Unfortunately Mona's taste is not so amusing in its threat to Poynton, and Mrs. Gereth, shudderingly aware of the "aesthetic misery" ⁶ of the Brigstocks, pictures the future state of her

9. Preface to *The Spoils of Poynton; A London Life; The Chaperon,* Collected Novels and Tales (New York, Charles Scribner's Sons, 1908), *10,* xii.
1. Ibid., p. xiii.
2. *The Spoils of Poynton* (Boston and New York, Houghton, Mifflin & Co., 1897), p. 174.
3. Ibid., p. 50.
4. Ibid., p. 33.
5. Ibid., p. 6.
6. Ibid., p. 1.

beloved house under Mona's reign, "the maddening relics of Waterbath, the little brackets and pink vases, the sweepings of bazaars, the family photographs and illuminated texts, the 'household art' and household piety of Mona's hideous home." [7]

Fleda Vetch fits none of these categories. Brought up amidst the tasteless collections of her father, she still has a "passion for beauty," [8] and has even spent a year in Paris, "arming herself for the battle of life by a course with an impressionist painter." [9] Her natural taste is even good enough to satisfy the creator of Poynton. "Mrs. Gereth had really no perception of anybody's nature—had only one question about persons: were they clever or stupid? To be clever meant to know the marks. Fleda knew them by direct inspiration, and a warm recognition of this had been her friend's tribute to her character." [1] But Mrs. Gereth's judgment of her is superficial at best, for appreciation to Fleda is as much a matter of morals as of esthetics. It is not in her nature to be simply Mrs. Gereth's "priestess of the altar," [2] just as it is equally impossible for her to think of Poynton as merely a collection of valuable objects. Her keenly developed moral sensitivity sharply distinguishes her from the other characters, and when combined with her esthetic sensitivity it gives her necessary decisions their dramatic character.

To Mrs. Gereth the arts of Poynton have nothing to do with common and accepted codes of morality. When it becomes obvious that she will be unable to stop Owen and the hated Mona from taking possession of the house, she secretly removes all its treasures to Ricks, her own little house, for proper safekeeping and appreciation, even though, ironically enough, it means destroying the spacious unity which made Poynton so matchless. After the first shock of discovery, Fleda finds that Mrs. Gereth not only sees nothing immoral in the theft, but even thinks it a praiseworthy move. "The girl's dread of a scandal . . . diminished the more she saw how little vulgar avidity had to do with this rigor. It was not the crude love of possession; it was the need to be faithful to a trust and loyal to an idea. The idea was surely noble: it was that of the beauty Mrs. Gereth had so patiently and consummately wrought." [3] F. W. Dupee in a happy phrase calls her "a persuasive example of enlightened egotism." [4] The expression is just, for Mrs. Gereth does act by a law of her own. She can steal the spoils, or try every trick and stratagem to force Fleda and Owen together in marriage, yet her actions do not spring from an easy material selfishness. In her desire for

7. Ibid., p. 21.
8. Ibid., p. 85.
9. Ibid., p. 14.
1. Ibid., p. 165.
2. Ibid., p. 43.
3. Ibid., p. 53.
4. Dupee, *James*, p. 189.

the good of others as well as herself, and in her search for the esthetically desirable, her egotism is even attractive, and only faintly resembles that of Gilbert Osmond in *The Portrait of a Lady*.

To Fleda Vetch, however, even recognizing as she does the enlightened aims of Mrs. Gereth, the actions of the older woman must be in unbearable conflict with her own code of ethics. "She had . . . to recognize that there were things for which Mrs. Gereth's *flair* was not so happy as for bargains and 'marks.' "[5] The moral question involved in the undeniable theft is as important to Fleda as the appreciation and enjoyment of the objects themselves. When she finds on her first visit to the now resplendent Ricks that Mrs. Gereth has given her a room furnished with the spoils, she can no longer enjoy them as she formerly did at Poynton. "She couldn't care for such things when they came to her in such ways; there was a wrong about them all that turned them to ugliness."[6] It becomes increasingly clear to her, as it did to Isabel Archer, that esthetic enjoyment divorced from morality is not enough: "The girl had hours, now, of sombre wishing that she might never see anything good again: that kind of experience was evidently not an infallible source of peace."[7] The immediate problem involved in this moral recognition quickly becomes apparent, and the new temptation to enjoy without thought and without conscience provides the thematic center of the novel.

For someone with a sensitive conscience but, unlike Fleda, with no passion for beauty, the solution to the problem would seem obvious. But Fleda's esthetic sensibilities deny any easy decision to force the return of the spoils. When she learns too that Mona is making the return a preliminary condition to her marriage to Owen, the problem becomes hopelessly involved. For Fleda is in love with Owen, and knows that he is at least partially in love with her, yet she cannot find it in her conscience to separate him from his fiancée by any deliberate act. This new conflict of love and morality is inseparably bound to the continued conflict of esthetics and morality, and the two reinforce each other. Mrs. Gereth partly understands the situation, and Fleda, refusing as much as possible to make any decision at all, can only return to her shabby home, leaving her friend to settle matters without advice or influence. There seems to her no other possible course; as she later tells Owen, " 'In the midst of those trophies of Poynton, living with them, touching them, using them, I felt as if I were backing her up.' "[8]

Mrs. Gereth, still hoping for the marriage between Fleda and Owen, does settle matters with one magnificent gesture. She returns the spoils

---

5. *Poynton*, p. 156.
6. Ibid., p. 92.
7. Ibid., pp. 165–6.
8. Ibid., p. 186.

to Poynton, even the little Maltese cross which suggests so indirectly the nature of the struggle. The gesture is in keeping with her character, and has been long prepared for by the emphasis on her unselfish love of the spoils: "Fleda distinguished as never before the purity of such a passion; it made Mrs. Gereth august and almost sublime. It was absolutely unselfish—she cared nothing for mere possession. She thought solely and incorruptibly of what was best for the things; she had surrendered them to the presumptive care of the one person of her acquaintance who felt about them as she felt herself, and whose long lease of the future would be the nearest approach that could be compassed to committing them to a museum." [9] It is the irony of the novel that by this act she unknowingly destroys any hopes that Mona will abandon Owen, and so destroys her hope that Fleda will have the care of Poynton, the hopes on which her decision was based. The act is more unselfish than Mrs. Gereth could guess.

By this gesture too she satisfies Fleda's moral scruples. With her conscience clear again, Fleda finds all of her old love of the beautiful returning:

> The loss was a gain to memory and love; it was to her too, at last, that, in condonation of her treachery, the old things had crept back. She greeted them with open arms; she thought of them hour after hour; they made a company with which solitude was warm and a picture that, at this crisis, overlaid poor Maggie's [her sister's] scant mahogany. It was really her obliterated passion that had revived, and with it an immense assent to Mrs. Gereth's early judgment of her. She too, she felt, was of the religion, and like any other of the passionately pious she could worship now even in the desert.[1]

For one short time, when Owen offers her the choice of any object in Poynton, she even enjoys the pleasure of possession, until that pleasure is cruelly cut short by the fire which destroys the house. Poynton is now gone forever, just as Owen is lost to her forever, but Fleda needs no possessions; her sensitivity to beauty, in presence or in recollection, has returned in strength. The price paid for contentment of her moral sense has been great, but it has brought again correspondingly great pleasure.

Mrs. Gereth too, after paying the cost of Mona's conscience, finds renewed pleasure. For her memory at least, as well as for Fleda's, she has satisfied the esthetic sense by making Poynton again "a single splendid object."[2] But more important, with the struggle to make a thing of

9. Ibid., p. 258.
1. Ibid., p. 285.
2. Ibid., p. 16.

beauty of the unpromising little Ricks she regains the artistic spirit which had enabled her first to create Poynton. Fleda can at last say again in all honesty, " 'Where on earth did you put your hand on such beautiful things?' " [3] The beauty of this new art is different from the art of Poynton which was measured by "marks" and "periods," and seemed to call only for "Buddhistic contemplation." [4] Mrs. Gereth's new art is even a greater one, for it carries in it now the values of life as well as the values of visual beauty. Even the maiden aunt to whom Ricks once belonged—a woman who also suffered—seems still present in spirit, and her presence adds a new beauty to the house. "The ghosts," Fleda calls this added feeling of human values and human history as she points out the new beauty to Mrs. Gereth. " 'Somehow there were no ghosts at Poynton,' Fleda went on. 'That was the only fault.' " [5]

The final situation would seem hardly that of comedy: Mona and Owen in a marriage doomed to misery, Mrs. Gereth deprived of her beloved Poynton, and Fleda left to a life of loneliness. Yet Mrs. Gereth and Fleda, too sensitive for the crude and predatory world in which they must live, have at last found their strength; after their moment of recognition they know finally where true happiness lies. The role of the visual arts in the novel makes the final self-knowledge explicit, and forbids misunderstanding of the profoundly moral character of the story. That central group of James' novels which began with *The Portrait of a Lady*, a group in which the theme of the moral-esthetic conflict is dramatically illustrated in all its complexity, reaches a fitting conclusion, and even a climax, in *The Spoils of Poynton*. With its success, James was ready to turn from a concentration on the single theme to experiments in technique, form, and matter which would eventually lead to those three great novels in which, in final synthesis, the theme of the central group becomes an integral element of the theme of the first.

3. Ibid., p. 300.
4. Ibid., p. 176.
5. Ibid., p. 303.

5

The Experiments and the Conjunction of Themes

THE final group of James' novels finds its strength and its fulfillment in *The Wings of the Dove* (1902), *The Ambassadors* (1903), and *The Golden Bowl* (1904). But these long and formidable novels were preceded by a number of shorter ones marking a transition between the two earlier individual themes and their final literary conjunction. *The Other House* (1896), *What Maisie Knew* (1898), *The Awkward Age* (1899), *The Sacred Fount* (1901), and even, in continuation, the late novel *The Outcry* (1911) may all be considered in some degree experimental novels, experimental at least in that James was introducing in them new means of enlarging his particular art of the novel. The dramatic form, the "reflector" presentation, the technique of the prying observer, and the so-called "late style," all techniques of fiction latent in his earlier work, are here deliberately used at length, first in these transitional novels, and finally, and with much surer success, in the three great novels at the end of the group.

Writing to H. G. Wells in 1902, James said that he would never again send a "copious preliminary statement" to an editor, and went on to say, "The relief, and greater intellectual dignity, so to speak, of working on one's own scale, one's own line of continuity and in one's own absolutely independent *tone,* is too precious to me to be again forfeited." [1] The remark explains much in the later novels, particularly the "style" to which so many object, for James was at last writing to satisfy his own artistic demands rather than those of an editor. In a moment of pique he could even say, in an unpublished letter, "Of the huge, base *bêtise* of the public I don't permit myself fatally to *think:* I shall do that only on my deathbed—when I can afford to." [2] The experimental novels with their honesty of dedication to the artistic problem provide a means of watching James grope toward his "absolutely independent *tone,*" and in them he seems momentarily more interested in developing a personal technique of fiction than in achieving a closely integrated and deeply felt presentation of life.

In *The Wings of the Dove, The Ambassadors,* and *The Golden Bowl* the new means are fully assimilated, and the final result rises far above mere virtuosity of technique. But more than a successful applica-

---

1. To H. G. Wells, Nov. 15, 1902, in *Letters, 1,* 406.
2. To William H. Fullerton, Dec. 13 [1890's] in HL.

tion of new methods, they also show the "line of continuity" of which James wrote in his letter to Wells. For the theme of the moral decision, as in the second group of novels, is at the center of each novel, and provides the primary interest of the story. But in addition to his continuation of the moral theme, James adds to it in these last novels a renewed interest in the theme of the American-European contrast so carefully defined in his first novels. He is no longer so interested in establishing the contrast or in commenting upon it, and his emphasis is relatively much lighter than in the earlier novels. But the theme is there once again, now an integral part of the moral problem, and points to the climactic nature of the three novels. As in earlier novels too, and to a much greater degree, the arts again provide a system of observation and a means of interpretation. The "line of continuity," in more than its obvious aspects, carries the reader and the critic as well as James himself forward to the final achievements.

Before that climax, however, came the experiment that began in *The Other House* and continued later in *The Awkward Age* and *The Outcry*. In working out the preliminary details of *The Other House* in the Notebook for December 26, 1893, James speaks of "the 1st chapter of my story—by which I mean the 1st act of my play!" [3] The remark is pertinent for it shows the degree to which he had committed this plot to the theater. The Notebook, in fact, outlines a three-act play, and it was from such a preliminary dramatic plan that the final novel grew. *The Outcry*, even more directly, is a three-act play hastily converted by a few narrative details into a novel. Even without specific knowledge of the genesis of the novels, however, the dramatic quality of the final result would be readily apparent. The restriction to a very few settings, the carefully marked entrances and exits, the emphasis on conversation, and the lack of a rich imagery outside of the conversations all point to the deep influence of the drama on the novel. The influence was, of course, to continue throughout the rest of James' life, but was never again to control so absolutely the form and content.

While revising the original dramatic plan for *The Other House* in 1909, making of the plan the play for which it was originally intended, James bewailed "the utterly last intense reductions and compressions," and "the mere vulgar anatomy and bare-bones poverty to which one has to squeeze it more and more." [4] The same economy is apparent in these "experimental" novels as well, leaving little of the proliferation of imagery to be seen later. In keeping with the methods of the theater, however, the setting for each scene of *The Other House* is given considerable attention, and the two houses which form the visual background

---

3. *The Notebooks of Henry James*, ed. F. O. Matthiessen and K. B. Murdock (New York, Oxford University Press, 1947), p. 139.
4. To Mrs. W. K. Clifford, July 19, 1909, in *Letters*, 2, 129.

of the novel do serve to put stress on the contrasts established by the story. The use is not that of characterization and definition, of the sort seen in *The American* or *The Europeans* or *The Portrait of a Lady*, but rather of emphasis, an emphasis perhaps best described by one character in the story: "She perceived once for all how the difference of the setting made another thing of the gem." [5] The novel is a story of intrigue, evil, and terror, and the center of this evil is "the other house," Tony Bream's mansion, characterized by its showy hall: "Bright, large and high, richly decorated and freely used, full of 'corners' and communications, it evidently played equally the part of a place of reunion and of a place of transit. It contained so many large pictures that if they hadn't looked somehow so recent it might have passed for a museum." [6] The ornate house is a fitting scene, almost in the tradition of Poe, for acts of mystery and terror.

In contrast to this splendid pile stands the "great, clean, square solitude" [7] of the house of Mrs. Beever and Jean Martle, the innocent observers of the evil to which they are unwittingly exposed. The furnishings are good, but ironically, only because they are old enough to have come back into fashion again. "Her mahogany had never moved, but the way people talked about it had, and the people who talked were now eager to sit down with her on everything that both she and they had anciently thought plainest and poorest." [8] This house represents stability and peace and natural order, taking much of its very tranquillity from the contrast offered by the showy and splendid "other house." Books Two and Three, corresponding to the final acts of the three-act play, take place entirely in this setting. The growing awareness of the evil taking form, culminating finally in the murder of a child and the proven guilt of the mysterious Rose Armiger, is felt only against the background of quiet and order furnished by the house. The intrigue and crime find their origin in that ornate house across the river, but are seen only here, in all their incongruity, destroying an atmosphere of simplicity and decency. In this dramatically effective contrast, visual as well as spiritual, the arts find their principal interpretative value in *The Other House,* and serve to indicate the single-mindedness with which James approached the experiment in dramatic form.

In contrast to this melodrama, *The Outcry* is an amusing little thing, and even in its comedy fits remarkably well the thematic patterns illustrated by the arts in the more serious novels, a reminder that in its final form it appeared after the three climactic novels. The plot is constructed around the problem of whether an impoverished English nobleman

5. *The Other House* (New York, Macmillan Co., 1896), p. 19.
6. Ibid., p. 12.
7. Ibid., p. 3.
8. Ibid., p. 318.

should sell a valuable painting from the family collection to a loud American millionaire, or whether he should preserve it for the nation. The American Mr. Bender with his " 'Eight thousand—slap down,' " [9] his great omnipresent checkbook, his ferocious acquisitiveness, and his frank vulgarity represents America in the novel, and suggests a caricature of some of the qualities of Christopher Newman of *The American* or Mr. Verver of *The Golden Bowl*. As a product of the land " 'where the eagle screams like a thousand steam-whistles and the newspapers flap like the leaves of the forest,' " [1] he is interested in art only when its price is high enough to bring him fame. " 'Bender simply can't *afford* not to be cited and celebrated as the biggest buyer who ever lived.' " [2] As an individual he is a source of amusement, but the more sensitive characters see in him a distinct threat to the real treasure of their country, a forecast of " 'more and more Benders to come: such a conquering horde as invaded the old civilisation, only armed now with huge chequebooks instead of with spears and battle-axes.' " [3]

Lord Theign's Dedborough Place, on the other hand, "still breathing the quiet air and the fair pannelled [sic] security of the couple of hushed and stored centuries," [4] represents all the age and the tradition which Mr. Bender is plundering. "An ancient, an assured elegance seemed to reign; pictures and preserved 'pieces,' cabinets and tapestries, spoke, each for itself, of fine selection and high distinction; while the originals of the old portraits, in more or less deserved salience, hung over the happy scene." [5] The irony of this thematic contrast is just that the Europeans who are most vociferous about the meaning of art are the ones most anxious to sell. Lord Theign makes a great pretence of scorning American money, but his loss of the fortune which the Mantovano would have brought is a sharp blow. The lowest creature of the novel is the effete and repellent Lord John who introduces Bender, obviously for a fee, to the galleries of his friends. " 'What values are *not* pecuniary?' " [6] he asks, reducing all the pretensions of the others to a lowest common denominator, and suggesting the relevance to the theme of the now familiar moral problem.

Young Hugh Crimble, to make the theme even more apparent, considers the projected sale as much a matter of morality as of economics or esthetics:

> "Ah, the Despoilers!" said Crimble with strong expression. "But it's *we*," he added, "who are base."

9. *The Outcry* (New York, Charles Scribner's Sons, 1911), p. 18.
1. Ibid., p. 219.
2. Ibid., p. 221.
3. Ibid., p. 131.
4. Ibid., p. 3.
5. Ibid., p. 4.
6. Ibid., p. 84.

" 'Base'?"—and Lord John's surprise was apparently genuine. "To want only to 'do business,' I mean, with our treasures, with our glories." [7]

He finds happy reinforcement in his love, Lady Grace, who can say, " 'Other people do other things—they appear to have done them, and to be doing them, all about us. But *we* have been so decently different—always and ever. We've never done anything disloyal.' " [8] Her word "disloyal" carries all the weight of the little dramatic comedy, for the whole corrupted group in selling their art treasures are disloyal to their society, to their country, to their professed ideals, and even to their family traditions. The very corruption, within its careful setting, is relevant to James' thematic "line of continuity" in a manner in which that of *The Other House* is not. But in relation to the experimental progress, both novels illustrate the development of a central theme by means of dramatic action, dramatic in an almost literal sense.

Similarly, in *The Awkward Age* the story is presented in an essentially dramatic fashion, although the novel was not, like *The Outcry* or *The Other House,* originally planned as a play, and is less openly influenced by the stage. In answer to a bewildered reader, James wrote:

> A work of art that one has to *explain* fails in so far, I suppose, of its mission. I suppose I must at any rate mention that I had in view a certain special social (highly "modern" and actual) London group and type and tone, which seemed to me to se prêter à merveille to an ironic—lightly and simply ironic!—treatment, and that clever people at least would know who, in general, and what, one meant. . . . The *form,* doubtless, of my picture is against it —a form all dramatic and scenic—of presented episodes, architecturally combined and each making a piece of the building; with no going behind, no *telling about* the figures save by their own appearance and action and with explanations reduced to the explanation of everything by all the other things *in* the picture.[9]

In the Preface to the novel he stresses as a corollary to these ideas the importance of "really constructive dialogue, dialogue organic and dramatic, speaking for itself, representing and embodying substance and form." [1] *The Awkward Age* then, although not so immediately a product of James' interest in the stage, does show a continuing attempt to make use of dramatic techniques in the novel.

7. Ibid., p. 51.
8. Ibid., p. 167.
9. To Miss Henrietta Reubell [Nov. 12, 1899], in *Letters, 1,* 333.
1. Preface to *The Awkward Age,* Collected Novels and Tales (New York, Charles Scribner's Sons, 1908), *9,* xiii.

The dramatic method, however, offered a particular problem for Henry James. A consistent imagery or symbolism requires one controlling mind capable of finding in the welter of events a unified pattern of meaning or appearance. In his use of the dramatic method, James denies his own overt, articulate control, or at least his own comments and explanations, and by not employing the strict "reflector technique" he fails to provide a corresponding central intelligence. With each character in the novel speaking only for himself (and in this novel it sometimes seems only to himself), a consistency and unity of imagery within the bounds of the realistic novel is most difficult to obtain. In addition, in concentrating on the new technique, James apparently cut himself loose momentarily from his earlier themes. As the subject expands, "swathed," as Carl Van Doren says, "in such countless folds of reference and gossip that, artfully as the drama is expounded, it comes to the ear with a muffled sound, like agreeable voices heard speaking at a distance which lets the actual words die away on the wind," [2] the novel becomes increasingly entangled until the exact theme is, in fact, indecipherable.

From time to time, of course, there are familiar touches. Old Mr. Longdon, for instance, like Rip Van Winkle returned from the past, provides a comparison and a contrast which heightens the ironic view of the very modern little social group of the novel. His country house, as his peculiar background, suggests an age and a tradition lacking in the modern house:

> Beyond the lawn the house was before him, old, square, red-roofed, well assured of its right to the place it took up in the world. This was a considerable space . . . and the look of possession had everywhere mixed with it, in the form of old windows and doors, the tone of old red surfaces, the style of old white facings, the age of old high creepers, the long confirmation of time. Suggestive of panelled rooms, of precious mahogany, of portraits of women dead, of colored china glimmering through glass doors, and delicate silver reflected on bared tables, the thing was one of those impressions of a particular period that it takes two centuries to produce.[3]

In sharp contrast is the house, splendid in its own way, which a member of the new society takes for a few weeks of amusement. It has so little character, so few associations that, characteristically enough, the modern group doesn't even know who owns it:

---

2. Carl Van Doren, *The American Novel, 1789–1939* (rev. ed. New York, Macmillan Co., 1940), p. 182.
3. *The Awkward Age* (New York, Harper & Bros., 1899), p. 281.

"To whom, in point of fact, does the place belong?"

"I'm awfully ashamed, but I'm afraid I don't know. That just came up here," the girl went on, "for Mr. Van." . . .

"And Mr. Van couldn't tell?"

"He has quite forgotten—though he has been here before. Of course it may have been with other people," she added in extenuation. "I mean it mayn't have been theirs then any more than it's Mitchy's." [4]

As one character says of the house, and might almost equally well have said of the house of any of the group, " 'It's a handsome compliment. He doesn't care what he does. It's his way of amusing himself.' " [5]

The problem, however, of articulate control within the dramatic presentation, allowing thematic development by a unified imagery, James attacked directly in one of these "experimental" novels. The success of *What Maisie Knew*, one of the great tours de force of literature, lies in its absolute faithfulness to the limited and innocent vision of the young Maisie. "To that then I settled—to the question of giving it *all*, the whole situation surrounding her, but of giving it only through the occasions and connexions of her proximity and her attention; only as it might pass before her and appeal to her, as it might touch her and affect her, for better or worse, for perceptive gain or perceptive loss." [6] Every event and every action of the novel is seen only by and through her immature mind, every articulated thought is hers, even though she herself is not the narrator of the story. Such full and consistent use of the "reflector technique," foreseen in earlier novels but never before so thoroughly exploited, provides the technical innovation of the novel. But a full knowledge of the arts, perhaps even a strong interest in them, is a matter of maturity. Since it would be out of character, and even a little ridiculous, for Maisie to think in terms of the formal arts, a positive lack of reference to them is a necessity to the new technique in this particular novel, and even provides, in an indirect manner, a certain interpretative value.

When in the novel Maisie finds herself idly interested in the madonnas of the National Gallery or the great golden madonna of Boulogne,[7] James' control of the experimental form is not denied, but rather his grasp of psychological realism, operating within the form, is even more firmly established. To a little girl hated by one mother and cynically made use of by another, the madonna image would naturally evoke

4. Ibid., p. 183.
5. Ibid., p. 187.
6. Preface to *What Maisie Knew; In the Cage; The Pupil*, Collected Novels and Tales (New York, Charles Scribner's Sons, 1908), *11*, x.
7. *What Maisie Knew* (Chicago and New York, Herbert S. Stone & Co., 1897), pp. 143, 348.

EXPERIMENTS AND CONJUNCTION 85

an instinctive fascination. Or again, Maisie is aware, realistically enough, of the minor household arts about her. Mrs. Farange, whom James calls in the *Notebooks,* "the painted Idol, the sharp, showy, fiercely questioning mamma," [8] is all too clearly a person of paint and stuffs to Maisie. From the beginning of the novel the girl is conscious of "her ladyship's remarkable appearance, her violent splendor, the wonderful color of her lips, and even the hard stare, like that of some gorgeous idol described in a story-book, that had come into her eyes in consequence of a curious thickening of their already rich circumference." [9] Those painted eyes fascinate Maisie, and remind one of the horrors of the childhood of David Copperfield: "Maisie received in petrifaction the full force of her mother's huge painted eyes—they were like Japanese lanterns swung under festive arches." [1] The ironic comment which these references make, however, arises not in the consciousness of Maisie, but in the consciousness of the reader, in the greater understanding which he can bring to the events seen by Maisie, who in her innocence and good faith cannot interpret the evil contained in them. Her understanding is confined severely within the limits of what she could know, but the reader's is free to reach far out of the limitation.

In *The Sacred Fount,* on the other hand, with the dramatization of the efforts not of a young, naïve girl but of a mature and experienced man to understand events and relations which defy easy analysis or direct understanding, the method is similar but the situation is almost reversed. The form is now that of the first person narrator, although, in keeping with earlier experiments in dramatic technique, thoughts are again expressed almost entirely in conversation. The story, simply enough, is the attempt by this narrator during the short period of a house party to discover the relationships between the other guests, using the relative individual changes in vigor and youthfulness as the key to understanding. The primary emphasis of the novel, however, is placed not on the relationships between the guests or on the moral or emotional questions involved, but on the perception and hesitating interpretation of the narrator. His thought processes are the true substance of the novel, and the only clues to these thoughts are in his conversation. But unlike *What Maisie Knew,* the conversation is so rooted in his hidden and subtle intelligence that it is often scarcely intelligible. Now it is the fictional character who understands and not the reader. Complete success with the new "prying observer" was to come only in later novels when the form was shifted back to the third-person "reflector" method of narration already achieved in *What Maisie Knew,* the form so ably discussed by Percy Lubbock in *The Craft of Fiction.*

8. *Notebooks,* p. 259.
9. *Maisie,* pp. 87–8.
1. Ibid., p. 183.

In *The Sacred Fount,* unfortunately, the method gives validity to all the parodies, quips, and sarcasms which have been directed against James since the first appearance of his "late style." The constant hinting at meaning, the refusal to state even indirections directly and intelligibly, the extreme sensitivity of reported conversation to meanings hidden from the reader, are together exasperating and tiresome. One soon loses patience with a narrator who thinks he speaks for his reader as well as for himself when he says, "It could *not* but be exciting to talk, as we talked, on the basis of those suppressed processes and unavowed references which made the meaning of our meeting so different from its form." [2] In the later novels, handled with more thought and precision, the technique takes on meaning and value, and is, in fact, an unavoidable method of presenting the chosen matter and the chosen perceptive mind. In *The Sacred Fount* it often seems little more than an ornate screen carelessly erected about the minute nucleus of matter and meaning.

James himself was aware of the shortcomings of the experiment, and betrays his awareness now and again in the reported conversation. The inevitable impression of the narrator as a moral peeping Tom, for instance, is early recognized:

> "To nose about for a relation that a lady has her reasons for keeping secret—"
>
> "Is made not only quite inoffensive, I hold"—he immediately took me up—"but positively honourable, by being confined to psychologic evidence."
>
> I wondered a little. "Honourable to whom?" [3]

This unintentional effect is a minor matter, however, much like the inevitable appearance of egotism conveyed by the letter writer in Richardson's epistolary novels, and may be excused as an unfortunate result of the technique. At one point in *The Sacred Fount,* on the other hand, a character asks the narrator, " 'How on earth can I tell what you're talking about?' " [4] and the reader echoes the question. As Mrs. Brissenden later says to the narrator, " 'With your art of putting things, one doesn't know where one is—nor, if you'll allow me to say so, do I quite think *you* always do.' " [5] There is a decided lack of rigorous organization or careful communication of meaning in the novel, a quality foreign to most of James' work, and the narrator's statement, "There are impressions too fine for words . . . ," [6] is disturbingly reminiscent of James' excuse of the "ineffable" in *Roderick Hudson.*

2. *The Sacred Fount* (New York, Charles Scribner's Sons, 1901), p. 272.
3. Ibid., pp. 65–6.
4. Ibid., p. 205.
5. Ibid., p. 262.
6. Ibid., p. 137.

One use of the arts [7] illustrates something of the confusion of the novel. At the beginning of the story the group of people assembled finds a remarkable portrait of a young man in black with a pale, lean, almost ghastly face, holding in his hand a somewhat obscure mask of a human face. There is some speculation over its meaning, and it is suggested that it be called "The Mask of Death." But the narrator has a better suggestion: " 'Isn't it much rather the Mask of Life? It's the man's own face that's Death. The other one, blooming and beautiful . . . is Life, and he's going to put it on; unless indeed he has just taken it off.' " [8] The symbolism, so reminiscent of Hawthorne, is immediately apparent, for the narrator of the story itself bases his decisions about the relations between guests on the amount of "life" one has taken from another to increase a personal lack of vitality. When it is decided by the group that the faces in the picture suggest those of two of the guests whose relations are in question, the symbolism is even more explicit. But after the successful creation of such a symbol, one capable of concentrating within itself the whole of the story, it is dropped from sight, its possibilities only half exploited.

The imagery of the arts has more interpretative value in terms of the experimental technique of the novel, the attempt of the narrator to understand and to analyze for himself and for the reader. He says of one character, for instance, "It took me but a minute then to add him to my little gallery— . . . the museum of those who put to me with such intensity the question of what had happened to them." [9] Each character within the new technique is a person to be carefully scrutinized, to be interpreted, to be imaginatively reconstructed. The *objet d'art*, requiring the same mental process, provides a most fitting comparison. Similarly, even James' terminology of the arts, used throughout all his writing, takes on an added dimension. His common use of the word "picture" to mean "scene" or "surroundings" or even "situation," for instance, offers a new interpretative source: "A couple of hours thus passed, and fresh accessions enriched the picture." [1] The complex interrelation of sight and understanding, of visual comprehension and intellectual comprehension, provides the basis of the new experiment, and the visual arts by their very nature, particularly in James' view of their suggestive quality, are completely fitting for their new use.

With the old and the new so mingled and even confounded in *The Sacred Fount,* the novel provides a convenient transition to the three great novels to follow. Its experimental quality, seen in the partial abandonment of the older techniques and the partial grasping of the new,

---

7. Cf. Leon Edel, Introductory Essay, *The Sacred Fount* (New York, Grove Press, 1953), pp. xvi–xx.
8. *Sacred Fount,* p. 56.
9. Ibid., p. 22.
1. Ibid., p. 13.

makes it a confusing and even annoying novel. Yet the experiment, like that of *The Other House* or *What Maisie Knew*, was not wasted, for it prepared the way for better work. Now James had borrowed from the stage a dramatic form for the novel, and had developed for its presentation the narrative technique of the "reflector," the highly observant, highly sensitive character devoted to penetrating and understanding the events about him, through whose filtering intelligence all events are seen. The period of experimentation was over, and James was ready to write the three great final novels which were to incorporate and to exploit his previous interests and his two pervasive themes.

The first published, although not the first written, was *The Wings of the Dove,* a novel, well worth a full criticism, which shows perhaps better than any other the value of the period of experimentation as well as the value of the earlier development of themes. In keeping with the new narrative technique, the novel opens with a scene reflected in the mind of Kate Croy, the girl who is to be a principal character and one of the several Jamesian reflectors of the novel. It is the room of her tawdry father. The "arm-chair upholstered in a glazed cloth that gave at once . . . the sense of the slippery and of the sticky," the "sallow prints on the walls," the "small lamp in coloured glass," the "purplish cloth on the principal table," [2] all give a sense of dingy poverty and of ugliness as disagreeable to the reader as to Kate. "What showed was the ugliness—so positive and palpable that it was somehow sustaining. It was a medium, a setting, and to that extent, after all, a dreadful sign of life." [3] When a short time later Kate visits her sister Marian, dull and complaining in her widowed poverty, the impression of "this hole" [4] is depressingly similar. James says in the Preface to the novel, "I had noted that there could be no full presentation of Milly Theale as *engaged* with elements amid which she was to draw her breath in such pain, should not the elements have been, with all solicitude, duly prefigured." [5] The elements prefigured in the first two books, as in this first scene, before Milly Theale herself appears in the novel, are more than the characters of the people who are to surround her; prefigured also is the atmosphere of ideas and appearances, ugliness and beauty, which is to play so important a part in the novel.

The sordid background in which Kate Croy sees her family even becomes a motivation for her, and so another element of which James speaks, when it is contrasted with the splendid background of "the tall,

2. *The Wings of the Dove* (2 vols. New York, Charles Scribner's Sons, 1902), *1,* 3.
3. Ibid., *1,* 14.
4. Ibid., *1,* 48.
5. Preface to *The Wings of the Dove,* Collected Novels and Tales (New York Charles Scribner's Sons, 1909), *19,* x–xi.

rich, heavy house at Lancaster Gate" [6] where she is living with her Aunt Maude. Here she finds wealth and luxury, and a correspondingly massive art, that make the rooms of her father and sister seem even uglier and more sordid. And the contrast increases, to her consciousness, a natural characteristic of her mind: "She saw as she had never seen before how material things spoke to her. She saw, and she blushed to see, that if, in contrast with some of its old aspects, life now affected her as a dress successfully 'done up,' this was exactly by reason of the trimmings and lace, was a matter of ribbons and silk and velvet. She had a dire accessibility to pleasure from such sources." [7] The "dire accessibility" in the face of the contrast offered by the two backgrounds, not unlike that of Hyacinth in *The Princess Casamassima,* gives an added urgency to the anguished pleas of her family not to lose the affection—and so the money—of Aunt Maude. With this powerful motivation so carefully established, the role of Kate Croy in the novel becomes more subtle and more sympathetic. The vigor with which she drives the reluctant Merton Densher to be "kind" to Milly Theale, and so inherit her fortune, Kate derives not from some overwhelming inherent evil but from the sharp contrast of beauty and ugliness, of wealth and poverty, acting on a certain moral weakness.

The contrast finds its strength not only in the physical background but in Aunt Maude as well. Her very appearance, in the eyes of Kate, carries a suggestion of the arts: "majestic, magnificent, high-coloured, all brilliant gloss, perpetual satin, twinkling bugles and flashing gems, with a lustre of agate eyes, a sheen of raven hair, a polish of complexion that was like that of well-kept china." [8] She in turn, like the Bellegardes of *The American,* also shows her character and her particular force in the setting in which she lives. She is in her own person a personification of Lancaster Gate and the pressure toward the life of wealth and ease which it represents for Kate. It is Merton Densher who best understands that she, almost impersonally, is keeping Kate from marrying him, and he too feels the pressure exerted in her house. "It was the language of the house itself that spoke to him, writing out for him, with surpassing breadth and freedom, the associations and conceptions, the ideals and possibilities of the mistress." [9] When he comes to ask Mrs. Lowder's consent to his engagement to Kate, he senses immediately that the difficulties, the impossibilities, facing him are as large as the house itself.

Densher reads the immensity of the problem before him in "the

---

6. *Wings of the Dove, 1,* 29.
7. Ibid., *1,* 31.
8. Ibid., *1,* 34.
9. Ibid., *1,* 87.

message of her massive, florid furniture, the immense expression of her signs and symbols." [1] For just as Aunt Maude provides for Kate a contrast to a world of poverty, she also provides for Densher a contrast to the moralistic world of thought of a poor reporter for whom the "want of means . . . was really the great ugliness" [2] and who simply wishes to marry the girl he loves:

> He had never dreamed of anything so fringed and scalloped, so buttoned and corded, drawn everywhere so tight, and curled everywhere so thick. He had never dreamed of so much gilt and glass, so much satin and plush, so much rosewood and marble and malachite. But it was, above all, the solid forms, the wasted finish, the misguided cost, the general attestation of morality and money, a good conscience and a big balance. These things finally represented for him a portentous negation of his own world of thought.[3]

The ironic phrase "morality and money" distinguishes the play of forces in Lancaster Gate, and defines the central theme. For it is within the conflict of these two values that the crime of Kate and the unwilling participation and eventual tragic recognition by Merton come into being. The house, representing Kate's hopes and Merton's fears, concentrates at one convenient point the thematic conflict of values which brings eventual failure, evil, and misery to them both.

In conjunction with that conflict, the theme of the European-American contrast is simultaneously present. Kate Croy belongs by nature to the world of Lancaster Gate, to the European world of wealth and appearances. It is her duty and her pleasure to represent "the artistic idea, the plastic substance" [4] imposed by the atmosphere of Lancaster Gate, and it is this natural affinity that gives that world such a power in the story. The American Milly Theale, when she appears, promptly recognizes the proper setting for her friend: "The handsome English girl from the heavy English house had been as a figure in a picture stepping by magic out of its frame." [5] Out of the picture for which she is so fitted, Kate seems unnatural and warped. It is fitting that James returned to the sister's house, "ugly almost to the point of the sinister," [6] for one of the final scenes of the novel. Through the eyes of Densher he puts emphasis again on one of the motives which has driven Kate through all the horror of the story; in that ugly squalor she is a stranger:

1. Ibid., *1*, 85.
2. Ibid., *1*, 70.
3. Ibid., *1*, 88.
4. Ibid., *2*, 37.
5. Ibid., *1*, 189.
6. Ibid., *2*, 396.

He had seen her but in places comparatively great—in her aunt's pompous house, under the high trees of Kensington and the storied ceilings of Venice. He had seen her, in Venice, . . . as the centre itself of the splendid Piazza: he had seen her there, . . . in his own poor rooms, which yet had consorted with her, having state and ancientry even in their poorness; but Mrs. Condrip's interior, even by this best view of it and though not flagrantly mean, showed itself as a setting almost grotesquely inapt.[7]

It is with great sensitivity that Densher feels there the point of the scene: "Kate wouldn't have been in the least the creature she was if what was just round them hadn't mismatched her." [8]

Once Milly Theale has entered this Europe whose "elements" are so carefully established, once she has been given her introduction, as it were, in England, and has reached Venice where the rest of her pathetically short life is to be lived, it is made increasingly clear that she too, American as she is, fits the background which she has deliberately chosen for herself. Her background, however, is not the massive, wealthy English house, but the old Venetian palace which she has rented, the beautiful Palazzo Leporelli. As her companion, Mrs. Susan Stringham, says, " 'She's lodged for the first time as she ought, from her type, to be; and doing it—I mean bringing out all the glory of the place—makes her really happy.' " [9] As Mrs. Stringham also suggests, and as Densher sees for himself, "This element gained from her, in a manner, for effect and harmony, as much as it gave." [1] The two elements of the picture interpret each other; to know one is to know the other. Such a close relationship constitutes one of James' means of indirect characterization, an outgrowth of his earlier direct comparison with the arts, and suggests the necessity of understanding what the arts mean to Milly herself. Her response to the arts, of which her response to the Palazzo Leporelli is simply a part, is one of the keys to her character, and in conjunction with Kate's view of Lancaster Gate is the explicit illustration of the theme of the relationship between esthetics and the higher morality, the theme that integrated with the American-European contrast makes the point of the story itself.

At Matcham, the great house of Lord Mark, Milly feels the general European atmosphere of the house and of the occasion, "a quantity expressed in introductions of charming new people, in walks through halls of armour, of pictures, of cabinets, of tapestry, of tea-tables, in an assault of reminders that this largeness of style was the sign of *appointed*

---

7. Ibid., *2,* 395.
8. Ibid., *2,* 396.
9. Ibid., *2,* 225.
1. Ibid., *2,* 202.

felicity." [2] It is the *"appointed* felicity" of the house and of the life which it represents that attracts Kate Croy. But Milly Theale, brought up in another atmosphere, must create her own felicity, must find her own meaning in life and the arts, and the difference in response to the house is just the difference in the two girls and in their two backgrounds. In contrast to Kate, Milly begins to find her own felicity as she gropes in the National Gallery for a personal meaning of the arts for her. Before this moment she had purposely avoided museums, but now she suddenly feels that she may have been neglecting great chances and great possibilities. Once in the halls, she knows that she is right. "It was the air she wanted and the world she would now exclusively choose; the quiet chambers, nobly overwhelming, rich but slightly veiled, opened out round her and made her presently say 'If I could lose myself here!' " [3]

In the gallery, in the magnificent art which surrounds her, she is able to forget herself, to merge her being—her fears as well as her hopes —in something greater than herself. "She really knew before long that what held her was the mere refuge, that something within her was after all too weak for the Turners and Titians. They joined hands about her in a circle too vast, though a circle that a year before she would only have desired to trace. They were truly for the larger, not for the smaller life." [4] The quality of escape and refuge which she finds there is a personal response drawn from her consciousness of the physical doom awaiting her, but the quality of the larger life suggested by the arts is one with which James was always concerned. The full weight of James' own view of the arts is pressing on Milly Theale. This moment of revelation in the National Gallery, however, moving though the moment may be, is but a preparation for the still greater revelations of Venice, and the still larger response to the arts.

The Palazzo Leporelli is itself a sort of personal gallery, and Densher even thinks to himself that time passes there "like a series of hours in a museum." [5] But it is more than a gallery; like the symbolic house of *The Sense of the Past* it is "a museum of held reverberations still more than of kept specimens." [6] Old, honored, beautiful, full of the art of the centuries, it stands as an intimate representative of the arts and of the life of Venice. It is not surprising that Milly finds in her "great gilded shell" [7] the same quality of refuge which she sensed in the National Gallery. She even expresses the thought aloud to Lord Mark when she

2. Ibid., *1*, 229.
3. Ibid., *1*, 314.
4. Ibid., *1*, 314-15.
5. Ibid., *2*, 188.
6. *The Sense of the Past,* ed. Percy Lubbock (New York, Charles Scribner's Sons, 1917), pp. 67-8.
7. *Wings of the Dove, 2,* 167.

repeats her "independent moral" that, "if one only had such a house for one's own and loved it and cherished it enough, it would pay one back in kind, would close one in from harm." [8] The refuge which it offers, however, in common with the National Gallery, is that of the larger life. "Palazzo Leporelli held its history still in its great lap, even like a painted idol, a solemn puppet hung about with decorations. Hung about with pictures and relics, the rich Venetian past, the ineffaceable character, was here the presence revered and served." [9] The significance is that of all great art for James, the suggestion of history, of tradition, of appreciation, of the full life. In the Palazzo Leporelli is felt the culmination of the meaning of the art of Europe so carefully defined, and even created, in James' earlier writing.

This suggestive, almost symbolic, quality of the art has a poignant and affecting meaning in *The Wings of the Dove,* for Milly knows that she is soon to die. She was born the charming and sensitive "potential heiress of all the ages," [1] but it is her will to live, her firm determination to enjoy as much of life as possible, that makes her courage attractive and her death tragic. And the art of Europe represents for her the full and undying life which she so desires; the Palazzo Leporelli with its history and tradition, its undying products of the human mind, is something greater and more lasting than the individual human life. It represents in its own way eternal life as well as full life. Within that meaning it is the refuge which Milly seeks, the refuge from ineffectual mortality. To remain within the palace is to remain within the stream of life: "She wouldn't let him call it keeping quiet, for she insisted that her palace—with all its romance and art and history—had set up round her a whirlwind of suggestion that never dropped for an hour. It wasn't, therefore, within such walls, confinement, it was the freedom of all the centuries." [2] With Milly thus living out the last of her days in this " 'expression of the pride of life,' " [3] James can portray her failing fortunes and her pathetic death by dramatic means without the critical dangers of direct description, and he makes full use of the opportunity.

The last public appearance which Milly makes, and the high point of her final struggle, is the great dinner which she gives in the palace. In her wonderful white dress, itself a gesture of defiance in keeping with the splendor of the rooms, she rejoices in those surroundings which set the tone of the gathering. She throws herself in desperation and joy into the full tide of life, acting under "an inspiration which was half her nerves and half an inevitable harmony." [4] The harmony is one she

---

8. Ibid., *2*, 175.
9. Ibid., *2*, 149.
1. Ibid., *1*, 122.
2. Ibid., *2*, 190.
3. Ibid., *2*, 161.
4. Ibid., *2*, 234.

cultivates, and as her end approaches she surrounds herself more and more with symbolic objects which bring her into relationship with the larger life. Coming to the palace on that night, Densher had particularly noticed the brilliant decorations: "He had found Susan Shepherd alone in the great saloon, where even more candles than their friend's large common allowance—she grew daily more splendid; they were all struck with it and chaffed her about it—lighted up the pervasive mystery of Style." [5] When at the end death has finally come, and Densher can only describe his last sight of her, it is a sight that recalls the brilliant evening, and shows Milly still fighting, still holding tight to the surroundings which mean so much to her:

> "Did she receive you—in her condition—in her room?"
> "Not she," said Merton Densher. "She received me just as usual: in that glorious great *salone,* in the dress she always wears, from her inveterate corner of her sofa." [6]

The vision alone illuminates the moment. If, as Milly early foresaw,[7] she had once lived as if she were dead, now she has died as if she were alive.

Long before her death, however, before seeing the Palazzo Leporelli at all, and even before going to the National Gallery, Milly sees at Matcham the great Bronzino portrait which she so closely resembles. The moment is one of the most telling of the novel: "The lady in question . . . with her slightly Michaelangelesque squareness, her eyes of other days, her full lips, her long neck, her recorded jewels, her brocaded and wasted reds, was a very great personage—only unaccompanied by a joy. And she was dead, dead, dead. Milly recognized her exactly in words that had nothing to do with her. 'I shall never be better than this.'" [8] In discussing this moment, F. O. Matthiessen remarks that James has thus transformed his heroine into a Renaissance princess, and goes on to say, "But at this exalted moment Milly also foresees that none of her happiness will last. Even as she looks, she realizes that the joyless lady on the canvas is 'dead, dead, dead'; and the words reverberate for us as an omen of her own future." [9] Matthiessen's remarks are acute, and show an awareness of the importance of the moment. To see in the portrait only an image of Milly as a princess, however, and to interpret her startling "dead, dead, dead" as only an omen of the future, is to miss much of the incisive meaning of the moment, particularly when Matthiessen continues in the next paragraph, "This scene

---

5. Ibid., *2,* 222.
6. Ibid., *2,* 356.
7. Ibid., *1,* 220.
8. Ibid., *1,* 242.
9. F. O. Matthiessen, *Henry James: the Major Phase* (New York, Oxford University Press, 1944), pp. 65–6.

before the Bronzino operates almost like a musical theme: it strikes the first note of the transition to Venice, where Milly plays out her make-believe rôle in the gorgeous rented palace which increases the ironic contrast 'between her fortune and her fear.' " [1]

The image of Milly as a Renaissance princess (and so a "make-believe rôle" in the palace) is certainly one element of the novel, but a minor one which only strengthens the more important thematic element defined by the arts. Matthiessen seems to have fallen into the same reading as F. W. Dupee who says of Milly, "She plays the 'princess' to everyone's fancy, although she does so in a rented palace many times too large for her small self and meager court." [2] The reading is disappointing, for much of the strength of the novel lies in just how well Milly does fit the palace, her private symbol which speaks with so ironic a smile of "a possible but forbidden life," [3] and just how meaningful she feels her life there to be. Her role is perhaps one of "make-believe," but not of self-deception. For it is the portrait and the palace which lead her to a recognition of how significant and how desirable life can be, yet how transient and how mortal her own is.

The Bronzino at Matcham is more than an image of Milly as a princess, and more than an omen of her death. The great lady of the portrait is "dead, dead, dead," and Milly is soon to be. Yet the lady, transmuted by art, not unlike the dancing nymph of *The Portrait of a Lady,* lives on and speaks to the living; she is greater than life and greater than death. James says, "Milly recognized her exactly in words that had nothing to do with her. 'I shall never be better than this.' " [4] But her word "this" is a most ambiguous reference. Lord Mark, within the world of the novel, thinks Milly is referring to the original lady of the portrait. Matthiessen believes she is referring to her own state of mind and general condition at that particular moment. But an equally possible interpretation, and one more in keeping, is that James' statement may mean, "Milly recognised the lady in the portrait exactly in words that had nothing to do with her. 'I shall never be better than this picture.' " For the portrait, like the pictures in the National Gallery or like the Palazzo Leporelli, represents a refuge from insignificance and mortality. It suggests the larger life, the fuller life which Milly is so courageously to seek.

Before the great portrait she had felt her supreme moment of joy, but at the instant of her anguished "dead, dead, dead" she had also felt her first and most telling moment of self-knowledge, the knowledge which was to carry her through to the end. The joy of the moment

1. Ibid., p. 66.
2. F. W. Dupee, *Henry James,* p. 255.
3. *Wings of the Dove,* 2, 162.
4. Ibid., 1, 242.

belongs to her introduction in the story; the anguish and the self-realization, to her total role. For the portrait gives her a first sight of the refuge and the challenge of the visual arts of Europe, the arts which within the novel are to symbolize her courage, her understanding, and her fears, the qualities which make her death such an affecting one. James had at last brought his technical experiments and his two carefully defined themes together in one great novel. The integration is an artistic success capable itself of establishing him as one of the great novelists in English, and furnishes a critical momentum which carries on through the two major novels to follow.

6

The Final Synthesis of Themes

THE two themes of the American-European contrast and the moral-esthetic relationship continue to meet in climactic interfusion in *The Ambassadors* and *The Golden Bowl*. In the earlier novel, the themes join most immediately in the consciousness of Strether, the "Jamesian reflector." "It had only been his charming office to project upon that wide field of the artist's vision—which hangs there ever in place like the white sheet suspended for the figures of a child's magic-lantern—a more fantastic and more moveable shadow."[1] Since the picture seen by the reader is Strether's personal projection, any discussion of the themes of the novel must in some degree be a discussion of his character. For as Strether increasingly feels within him the conflict of the restricting life he has left behind him and the enlarging life he sees potentially before him, his thoughts and his vision, illustrated in large part by the effect of the arts about him, are at the center of the moral problem. Yet the two sorts of life are dramatically represented and even defined by the memory of Woollett, Massachusetts, and the immense presence of Paris.

Paris, like the London of *The Wings of the Dove,* is defined in its houses. That of Madame de Vionnet, for instance, suggests at first "some glory, some prosperity of the first Empire, some Napoleonic glamour, some dim lustre of the great legend; elements clinging still to all the consular chairs and mythological brasses and sphinxes' heads and faded surfaces of satin striped with alternate silk."[2] Its associations are immense; like Ralph Pendrel's allegorical house in *The Sense of the Past,* it is "a piece of suggestive concrete antiquity."[3] Strether sees other houses which breathe the essence of Paris, notably those of Chad and Maria Gostrey, but none which have the same feeling of accumulated tradition. And equally important, the European Madame de Vionnet belongs to this background as much as it belongs to her; she is herself a living work of art. "Her head, extremely fair and exquisitely festal, was like a happy fancy, a notion of the antique, on an old, precious medal, some silver coin of the Renaissance."[4] The imagery

---
1. Preface to *The Ambassadors,* Collected Novels and Tales (New York, Charles Scribner's Sons, 1909), *21,* ix.
2. *The Ambassadors* (New York and London, Harper & Bros., 1903), pp. 169–70.
3. *The Sense of the Past,* p. 30.
4. *Ambassadors,* p. 188.

of her description drawn from the arts is rich and various, and even her daughter partakes of the quality: "She was fairly beautiful to him —a faint pastel in an oval frame; he thought of her already as of some lurking image in a long gallery, the portrait of a small old-time princess of whom nothing was known but that she had died young." [5] She is a living part of a deep and rich culture, an inheritance passed on through the ages.

The characterization, of course, is one which takes place in Strether's consciousness: "It was doubtless half the projection of his mind, but his mind was a thing that, among old waxed parquets, pale shades of pink and green, pseudo-classic candelabra, he had always needfully to reckon with." [6] The early English scenes, where "the wicked old Rows of Chester" [7] seem to him so meaningful, introduce the general concept of Europe in the novel, but it is the Paris where, as in Maria Gostrey's rooms, "the lust of the eyes and the pride of life had indeed thus their temple," [8] that forms the Europe of the novel, and offers such a contrast to the restricted Woollett left far behind in Massachusetts. The direct result of Strether's break with Woollett is in his actions, particularly his attempts to save Chad not from Paris, as he originally came to do, but from Woollett, yet the cause and even the measure of that break is in the growth of his understanding and appreciation of Paris.

If the "germ" of the moral theme is found in Strether's plea to Bilham to live the fullest possible life, the "germ" of the evocation of Paris and all it represents is found in the setting for that plea, the house and garden of Gloriani, the great artist whom James found suggested, interestingly enough, by the artist Whistler: [9]

> The place itself was a great impression—a small pavilion, clear-faced and sequestered, an effect of polished *parquet,* of fine white panel and spare, sallow gilt, of decoration delicate and rare, in the heart of the Faubourg Saint Germain and on the edge of a cluster of gardens attached to old noble houses. Far back from streets and unsuspected by crowds, reached by a long passage and a quiet court, it was as striking to the unprepared mind, he immediately saw, as a treasure dug up; giving him too, more than anything yet, the note of the range of the immeasurable town and sweeping away, as by a last brave brush, his usual landmarks and terms.[1]

Denying all that Strether had known before, it offers for his appreciative grasp a culture, a range of thought, and a tradition never before en-

5. Ibid., p. 180.
6. Ibid., pp. 288–9.
7. Ibid., p. 29.
8. Ibid., p. 82.
9. Cf. letter to W. D. Howells, Aug. 10, 1901, in *Letters, 1,* 376.
1. *Ambassadors,* p. 134.

countered. The full dignity of the human being past and present is there: "'It's always as charming as this; it's as if, by something in the air, our squalor didn't show. It puts us all back—into the last century.'"[2] There Strether, so sensitive to his surroundings, feels the need to make his emotional plea for youth and enjoyment and the full life.

Chad's balcony too, which plays such an interesting part in the novel, looks out over the whole city, and its position is almost symbolic. Time and again Strether looks down from a balcony or a window to feel the physical presence of the great city encircling him. The houses are so pervaded with the atmosphere of Paris that they become indistinguishable from that atmosphere. Even the rooms which the American Mrs. Pocock has taken cannot exclude it: "The glazed and gilded room, all red damask, ormolu, mirrors, clocks, looked south, and the shutters were bowed upon the summer morning; but the Tuileries garden and what was beyond it, over which the whole place hung, were things visible through gaps; so that the far-spreading presence of Paris came up in coolness, dimness and invitation."[3] This continual presence is perhaps most explicitly noted by Strether as he sits alone one evening in Chad's house: "The night was hot and heavy and the single lamp sufficient; the great flare of the lighted city, rising high, spending itself afar, played up from the Boulevard and, through the vague vista of the successive rooms, brought objects into view and added to their dignity."[4] The rooms of *The Ambassadors* all seem to open directly onto Paris, and to be always redolent of the scent of the city.

This pervading consciousness of atmosphere, within the world of the novel a product of Strether's mind, helps to make him also a sympathetic figure in the Paris scene, strange and foreign as that scene first appears to him. For, in keeping with James' own self-discovery in Europe, Strether increasingly tends to think in terms of "the picture." Even the other characters are seen as examples of the arts. Complete fulfillment of the metaphor is finally reached in the brilliant presentation of his day in the country, a vision, as Matthiessen has noted, conveyed explicitly in terms of an impressionist canvas. Strether's metaphor is particularly fitting, for "the high light of Paris, a cool, full studio-light, becoming, yet treacherous"[5] seems to demand a pictorial vision able to comprehend simultaneously the atmosphere of the city and its physical appearance. One is even reminded of the attempts of the impressionists to convey the quality and appearance of light when Miss Barrace explains this keen pictorial sense: "'I dare say . . . that I do, that we all do here, run too much to mere eye. But how can it be helped? We're all looking at each other—and in the light of Paris one sees what

2. Ibid., p. 138.
3. Ibid., pp. 267-8.
4. Ibid., p. 362.
5. Ibid., p. 254.

things resemble. That's what the light of Paris seems always to show. It's the fault of the light of Paris—dear old light!' " [6]

The quickened sense of visual impression, the suggestive value of houses and objects, the careful placing of characters in this background, all contribute to the atmosphere of the Paris of the novel. In James' preliminary résumé he had said of the scene of Strether's last meeting with Madame de Vionnet, "It is really the climax—for all it can be made to give and to do, for the force with which it may illustrate and illuminate the subject . . . ," [7] and it is only to be expected that the interpretative value of the arts should find a climax there as well. Fittingly enough, the scene begins with Strether's realization of the impressionistic world in which he is living: "Between nine and ten, at last, in the high, clear picture—he was moving in these days, as in a gallery, from clever canvas to clever canvas—he drew a long breath." [8] When he enters Madame de Vionnet's house he finds all of Paris there too: "From a great distance—beyond the court, beyond the *corps de logis* forming the front—came, as if excited and exciting, the vague voice of Paris." [9] His historic sense is again aroused, and he knows that this room and this scene are beyond anything that Madame de Vionnet could consciously create, for it is suggestive of "things from far back—tyrannies of history, facts of type, values, as the painters said, of expression." [1] Its center of interest, however, is the woman herself; "Strether in fact scarce knew what analogy was evoked for him as the charming woman . . . moved over her great room with her image almost repeated in its polished floor, which had been fully bared for summer." [2] She belongs so to this background, this evocation of the full meaning of Paris, that she not only lives in it, she is literally reflected in it. One is reminded of Thoreau's description of fishing on the clear and brilliantly reflecting Walden Pond, where the fish beneath and the birds above seem inseparably mingled under the surface. Madame de Vionnet and the impression of Paris are inseparably mingled in her house.

The Paris of Madame de Vionnet's house, however, does more than symbolize a culture and a way of life; it simultaneously continues the theme of the moral choice. In that magnificent last scene together, Madame de Vionnet says to Strether, " 'I've made a change in your life, I know I have; I've upset everything in your mind as well; in your sense of—what shall I call it?—all the decencies and possibilities.' " [3]

6. Ibid., pp. 142-3.
7. *The Notebooks of Henry James,* ed. Matthiessen and Murdock, p. 413.
8. *Ambassadors,* p. 396.
9. Ibid., p. 396.
1. Ibid., p. 397.
2. Ibid., p. 397.
3. Ibid., p. 401.

The choice of terms is admirable, for the story of the novel is just the conflict within the mind of Strether of all the decencies and the possibilities. In the mind of Woollett, representing the "New England conscience" [4] of which James speaks in the preliminary résumé, the decencies of the situation exist only in Strether's extracting Chad from Paris and returning to America as soon as possible. Any argument that Chad may be better off in Paris than at home seems immoral to Mrs. Pocock, the delegated representative of Woollett: " 'What is your conduct but an outrage to women like *us?* I mean your acting as if there can be a doubt—as between us and such another—of his duty?' " [5] To Strether, on the other hand, Paris represents the possibilities of life, the possibilities of greater spiritual achievement and the rediscovery of youthful *joie de vivre.* Between the two positions stands the symbol of Paris itself.

James was fully aware of the popular and trivial American idea of Paris, "the dreadful little old tradition, one of the platitudes of the human comedy, that people's moral scheme *does* break down in Paris." [6] This is the idea exploited by Mr. Pocock, the fictional forerunner of the American Legionnaire, and the idea which James uses with such effect to bolster Woollett's view—at least in the mind of Woollett—of the decencies of the situation. But James goes on in the Preface to say that by creating the character of Strether who lives only in intense reflection, the character is placed "very much *in* Paris, but with the surrounding scene itself a minor matter, a mere symbol for more things than had been dreamt of in the philosophy of Woollett." [7] The words "minor" and "mere" are puzzling, and suggest, as so often in the prefaces, that James was not always fully aware of what he had created. For the symbol of Paris, so carefully established in the novel, is exactly what gives validity to Strether's abandonment of the life and ideals of Woollett. The Paris of *The Ambassadors,* created to such a great extent by reference to the arts, is not the wicked city of the popular American view, nor is it the city of reality; it is a great poetic symbol expressing and vivifying the themes of the novel.

The two themes become one within this symbol, but in no awkward or exaggerated fashion. Strether's deep ethical sense, for instance, does not change, as it might in a more simplified plot. He slowly comes to defy Woollett's conception of duty, the restricted ethics of a world in which the arts are not an integral part of life, but his sense of essential morality remains. He may refuse to carry out his original mission, his duty Woollett would call it, but he is still morally repelled by the secret

4. *Notebooks,* p. 375.
5. *Ambassadors,* p. 342.
6. Preface to *Ambassadors,* pp. xiii–xiv.
7. Ibid., p. xiv.

intimacy between Chad and Madame de Vionnet, and he will accept no physical gain, in the person of Maria Gostrey, for his refusal. His esthetic sense on the other hand, applied to human life but controlled by the moral view, is changed immensely. And the change gives added significance to James' method of creating the symbol by the evocation of the arts. For beauty is a distinguishing characteristic of the physical Paris of the novel, and it is the beauty of the Parisian life that quickens Strether's sense of the greater morality, the duty of the spirit to find its highest expression.

Morality and the arts, the American atmosphere and the European, all intermingle in a close relationship which defines the theme of the novel, and in effect the complex theme of James' three final novels. The relationship is not a static one within the group, however, but varies from novel to novel. In *The Golden Bowl,* as in *The Wings of the Dove,* the elements of the theme are those of *The Ambassadors,* but the relationship between elements takes a new form. The European-American conflict is again an integral part of the theme and the background, and the story in essence is again the problem of the moral decision, defined and illustrated by the relationship between morality and esthetics. But the story is a new one, deserving of fuller treatment here, and the thematic development is in keeping with the new fictional situation. James was taking full advantage of the possibilities of his earlier themes by creating new combinations and new relationships, not simply by finding a new story to illustrate the old themes.

Yet in *The Golden Bowl* many of the thematic assumptions are by now familiar ones. The Prince is the only European by birth among the four principal characters. When his wife Maggie discovers his adulterous relationship with her young stepmother Charlotte, she knows that part of the responsibility for anything he does may be placed on his inherited traditions: "Such a place as Amerigo's was like something made for him beforehand by innumerable facts, facts largely of the sort known as historical, made by ancestors, examples, traditions, habits." [8] He is a product of the history of his illustrious Italian family, and is, imaginatively, himself present in "one of the ampler shrines of the supreme exhibitory temple, an alcove of shelves charged with the gold-and-brown, gold-and-ivory, of old Italian bindings and consecrated to the records of the Prince's race." [9] It is in keeping with James' earlier methods that the Prince, the product of such a formative European background, can be seen as a direct contrast to the American character, and can be approached through the arts of that European background to which he belongs.

Characteristically, a number of specific metaphors are applied to

8. *The Golden Bowl* (2 vols. New York, Charles Scribner's Sons, 1904), *2,* 331.
9. Ibid., *2,* 152-3.

him: "It was as if he had been some old embossed coin, of a purity of gold no longer used, stamped with glorious arms, mediaeval, wonderful." [1] Most commonly, they are architectural images: "The Prince's dark blue eyes were of the finest, and, on occasion, precisely, resembled nothing so much as the high windows of a Roman palace, of an historic front by one of the great old designers, thrown open on a feast-day to the golden air." [2] Perhaps the best known and most extended such image is that of a great Palladian church.[3] Even his moral sense, suitably enough, is like " 'the tortuous stone staircase—half-ruined into the bargain!—in some castle of our *quattrocento,*' " [4] so reminiscent of his own palace in Rome. For Amerigo—the name ironically suggests the European contrast—is, like Madame de Vionnet, an integral figure in his traditional background. At a reception in London, Charlotte Verver, his lover and the wife of his new father-in-law, feels that he makes the great house even grander: "When . . . she saw the Prince come back she had an impression of all the place as higher and wider and more appointed for great moments; with its dome of lustres lifted, its ascents and descents more majestic, its marble tiers more vividly overhung." [5] He belongs to the traditional world of the arts, and contributes to it his own splendor.

In the eyes of Mr. Verver, his father-in-law, the Prince is even a piece for the art collection which the American millionaire is making for his adopted town, American City. Maggie carefully points out the role: " 'You're at any rate a part of his collection, . . . one of the things that can only be got over here. You're a rarity, an object of beauty, an object of price.' " [6] Mr. Verver, representing in some respects the rising power of American wealth, has come to Europe, like Mr. Bender of *The Outcry,* "to rifle the Golden Isles." [7] But money is no source of pride to him; his pride is in the mastering of any doubt of his own esthetic facility, the unquestioning taste which produces his collection. The self-confidence, however, won with such difficulty, brings with it a familiar thematic confusion of esthetic and human judgment: "Representative precious objects, great ancient pictures and other works of art, fine eminent 'pieces' in gold, in silver, in enamel, majolica, ivory, bronze, had for a number of years so multiplied themselves round him and, as a general challenge to acquisition and appreciation, so engaged all the faculties of his mind, that the instinct, the particular sharpened appetite of the collector, had fairly served as a basis for his acceptance of the Prince's

1. Ibid., *1,* 23.
2. Ibid., *1,* 43.
3. Ibid., *2,* 3–5.
4. Ibid., *1,* 32.
5. Ibid., *1,* 248.
6. Ibid., *1,* 12.
7. Ibid., *1,* 142.

suit." [8] His replacement of human and even spiritual values with the esthetic—his museum is "a monument to the religion he wished to propagate" [9]—is not so complete as that of Gilbert Osmond in *The Portrait of a Lady,* but it does similarly lead to a failure to grasp the essential truths of human life.

Unlike Milly Theale of *The Wings of the Dove,* Mr. Verver finds in the arts no renewed sensitivity to life. It is difficult, in fact, to find any sensitivity at all. Since the Prince in the first half of the novel and Maggie in the second provide the filtering intelligences of the novel, in so far as the reflector technique is used, the mind of Mr. Verver is never seen directly or without prejudice, and the reader must depend upon the impressions gained by others. The others, however, are never sure of what he is feeling or even of how much he knows. Maggie, for instance, aware of the situation existing between her father and his unfaithful wife, asks, " 'Am I in the least sure that, with everything, he even knows what it is? And yet am I in the least sure he doesn't?' " [1] and she echoes the doubt of the reader. Even Mrs. Assingham, the prying observer who prides herself on seeing through any situation, remains in doubt:

> "You see he *may* be stupid too."
> "Precisely—there you are."
> "Yet on the other hand," she always went on, "he *may* be sublime: sublimer even than Maggie herself." [2]

He remains distant and secluded, as though separated from life, and Maggie, like the others, can only vainly dash herself against "the polished old ivory of her father's inattackable surface," [3] and "the firm outer shell of his dignity, all marvellous enamel." [4] The wall of esthetics and taste which he has erected between himself and the full tide of life is impenetrable.

Whatever his knowledge, Mr. Verver is incapable of normal human relations. The intimacy and love between himself and his daughter is not only faintly unpleasant, but precipitates much of the horror of the novel. Yet even in this relationship the father's esthetic sense rules his pleasure and his behavior. His description of their mutual happiness has an inhuman quality which damns him:

> "There seems a kind of charm, doesn't there? on our life—and quite as if, just lately, it had got itself somehow renewed, had waked up refreshed. A kind of wicked selfish prosperity perhaps, as if we had

8. Ibid., *1,* 141.
9. Ibid., *1,* 148.
1. Ibid., *2,* 182.
2. Ibid., *2,* 140.
3. Ibid., *2,* 308.
4. Ibid., *2,* 210.

grabbed everything, fixed everything, down to the last lovely object for the last glass case of the last corner, left over, of my old show. That's the only take-off, that it has made us perhaps lazy, a wee bit languid—lying like gods together, all careless of mankind." [5]

It is no wonder that in one of his few personal metaphors he thinks of her as "some slight, slim draped 'antique' of Vatican or Capitoline halls, late and refined." [6] He has no need of personal relationships; his taste gives him a large enough private life, and for acquaintances he can apply "the same measure of value to such different pieces of property as old Persian carpets, say, and new human acquisitions." [7]

He marries Charlotte ostensibly for the sake of Maggie, yet his relationship with his new wife takes the same form as that with his daughter. He is determined not to make the same mistakes he had made with his first wife: "The futilities, the enormities, the depravities, of decoration and ingenuity, that, before his sense was unsealed, she had made him think lovely!" [8] About this new wife, however, his esthetic sense reassures him; like the Prince, she is another piece for his collection: "He saw the sleeves of her jacket drawn to her wrists, but he again made out the free arms within them to be of the completely rounded, the polished slimness that Florentine sculptors, in the great time, had loved, and of which the apparent firmness is expressed in their old silver and old bronze." [9] The thought of marrying her is like the examination of a precious work of art: "He still but held his vision in place, steadying it fairly with his hands, as he had often steadied, for inspection, a precarious old pot or kept a glazed picture in its right relation to the light." [1] It does not take Charlotte long to understand this relationship, and she tries to play her part in it satisfactorily. "One of the attentions she had from immediately after her marriage most freely paid him was that of her interest in his rarities, her appreciation of his taste, her native passion for beautiful objects and her grateful desire not to miss anything he could teach her about them." [2] Even her flair for beautiful clothes and her delight in them, stressed so often throughout the novel, takes on a sinister air when seen in relation to the esthetic appreciation of a husband who leaves love to another man.

Despite the opinion of critics such as Caroline Gordon who find him "the best man James was able to imagine," [3] James seems fully aware

5. Ibid., *2*, 94.
6. Ibid., *1*, 190.
7. Ibid., *1*, 199.
8. Ibid., *1*, 144.
9. Ibid., *1*, 49.
1. Ibid., *1*, 213.
2. Ibid., *2*, 294.
3. Caroline Gordon, "Mr. Verver, Our National Hero," *Sewanee Review*, 63 (Winter, 1955), 45.

of the character he has created in Mr. Verver. Explicit moral judgment is not necessary, for in keeping with the moral theme Mr. Verver condemns himself. One need only note one of Maggie's final views of him: "He had ever, of course, had his way of walking about to review his possessions and verify their condition; but this was a pastime to which he now struck her as almost extravagantly addicted, and when she passed near him and he turned to give her a smile she caught—or so she fancied—the greater depth of his small, perpetual hum of contemplation." [4] The horror is only latent, for he is not yet, like Gilbert Osmond, spiritually and morally dead. Yet the danger is there, and James suggests it in a passage which recalls Walter Pater and the whole cult of estheticism: "It was all, at bottom, in him, the aesthetic principle, planted where it could burn with a cold, still flame; where it fed almost wholly on the material directly involved, on the idea (followed by appropriation) of plastic beauty, of the thing visibly perfect in its kind." [5] As yet the flame consumes only external materials, but it is constantly charring the internal as well.

The theme of the moral problem illustrated by Mr. Verver may then be approached, as in earlier novels, through the arts. The method reaches its most meaningful and its most original point in the central symbol of the golden bowl. The explicit implications of the symbol, as well as its basic structure and development, have been discussed most ably by F. O. Matthiessen. He points out James' use of the bowl "as a means of bringing to a focal point the varying and diverging complexities in . . . human relations," [6] and makes clear the relevance of the crack in the bowl to the "cracked" relations within the oddly compounded family. He shows particular insight in his discussion of the implications of wealth in the bowl, the gold of the bowl itself and "the mingled images of beauty and wealth" [7] with which the novel is filled. Finally, although its relevance to the symbol of the bowl is not directly stated, he discusses the tortured scene in which Charlotte, showing off to visitors the treasures of Mr. Verver's house, indirectly lectures on herself as well as the art. After his chapter there seems to be little need of further examination of the explicit symbolism of the bowl. Of the implicit significance of the bowl and of the arts in general, however, a great deal remains to be noted. Matthiessen is not particularly interested in the moral problem presented by *The Golden Bowl,* and it is that problem which provides the thematic center of the novel.

Maggie herself likes to use images drawn from the arts to describe situations, mental positions as it were, in which she finds herself. She plays with a comparison of her response at one moment to Charlotte and

4. *Golden Bowl, 2,* 294.
5. Ibid., *1,* 200.
6 Matthiessen, *Henry James: The Major Phase,* p. 83.
7. Ibid., p. 86.

the Prince, for instance, "as she might have played with a medallion containing on either side a cherished little portrait." [8] Or again, the sudden realization of the variety of attractions which Amerigo offers her suggests a similar image: "That was an old, old story, but the truth of it shone out to her like the beauty of some family picture, some mellow portrait of an ancestor." [9] Maggie is particularly fond of architectural images, and the great extended image by which she characterizes her complex family situation is developed at length: "This situation had been occupying, for months and months, the very centre of the garden of her life, but it had reared itself there like some strange, tall tower of ivory, or perhaps rather some wonderful, beautiful, but outlandish pagoda, a structure plated with hard, bright porcelain, coloured and figured and adorned, at the overhanging eaves, with silver bells that tinkled, ever so charmingly, when stirred by chance airs." [1] Similarly, she often visualizes the concerted schemes of Charlotte and the Prince in terms of buildings: "They had built her in with their purpose—which was why, above her, a vault seemed more heavily to arch." [2] Or again, "Verily it towered before her, this history of their confidence. They had built strong and piled high." [3] Even her own response to the two is made a part of the pattern when it is said of her denial of knowledge of Charlotte's actions, "It positively helped her to build up her falsehood—to which, accordingly, she contributed another block." [4]

The greater value of this imagery, however, lies in its relation to the complex character of Maggie herself. Early in the novel Charlotte says of her, "'She's not selfish enough,'" and goes on to develop her idea that Maggie can forgive the Prince anything so long as she loves him: "'Anything—anything that you might do and that you don't. She lets everything go but her own disposition to be kind to you.'" [5] This unselfishness is exemplified most obviously by her forbearance in the sickening complications of unfaithfulness and adultery in which she sees her husband and her stepmother. Her first response to the knowledge is not anger or even desire for revenge, certainly not a desire to die, but rather a desire to "live, live on somehow for their benefit, and even as much as possible in their company, to keep proving to them that they had truly escaped." [6] To the very end, generous as always, she lets Charlotte believe whatever will least hurt her, whatever will best allow the stepmother to retain her pride.

This extreme generosity, however, amounting even to self-effacement,

8. *Golden Bowl*, *2*, 37.
9. Ibid., *2*, 22.
1. Ibid., *2*, 3.
2. Ibid., *2*, 45.
3. Ibid., *2*, 200.
4. Ibid., *2*, 256.
5. Ibid., *1*, 105.
6. Ibid., *2*, 241.

is not entirely the admirable quality which so many critics have thought it. She has so little pride, so little desire to exert herself in the struggle; her very generosity becomes a form of selfishness, for she leaves the fight to others, supporting them for the sake of her own peace. She intends to remain, as Fanny Assingham has noticed in her character, "*'outside* of ugly things, so ignorant of any falsity or cruelty or vulgarity as never to have to be touched by them or to touch them.' "[7] Even in the world of society, the field of moral action in James' novels, she leaves the work to the Prince and Charlotte. Maggie avoids effort, avoids knowledge, avoids life itself. As her friend Fanny Assingham says, " 'She stands off and off, so as not to arrive; she keeps out to sea and away from the rocks.' "[8] She finds it easier and much more comfortable not even to know what is happening about her. Her conversation with Fanny, late in the novel, is almost a summary of Maggie's story:

> "I know nothing. If I did—!"
> "Well, if you did?" Fanny asked as she faltered.
> She had had enough, however. "I should die," she said as she turned away.[9]

Maggie herself is not evil; her life is devoted to avoiding even the knowledge of evil. Her generosity, her regard for the well-being of others, is a means of self-protection, an extended defense against the attack of life.

Maggie leads in effect an artificial life in a world carefully constructed by herself. "I live in the midst of miracles of arrangement, half of which I admit, are my own; I go about on tiptoe, I watch for every sound, I feel every breath, and yet I try all the while to seem as smooth as old satin dyed rose-colour.' "[1] In the light of such a consciousness the imagery of the arts in the novel takes on its added meaning. Even the art of dress, as Maggie implies, provides "a refuge, a beguilement."[2] Dress for her is a protection from any storm: to confront Fanny Assingham with her discovery of the Prince's unfaithfulness, Maggie carefully overdresses and bedecks herself with jewels. "These two items of her aspect had, promptly enough, their own light for Mrs. Assingham, who made out by it that nothing more pathetic could be imagined than the refuge and disguise her agitation had instinctively asked of the arts of dress."[3] Maggie's action is not surprising, however, for at moments of trial she instinctively seeks the arts. When her doubts of the true relation between her stepmother and her husband reach an unbearable stage, just

7. Ibid., *2*, 115–16.
8. Ibid., *2*, 136.
9. Ibid., *2*, 314.
1. Ibid., *2*, 114–15.
2. Ibid., *2*, 13.
3. Ibid., *2*, 158.

before the discovery of the golden bowl, she even goes to the museum and finds that there she can again believe in the Prince. "Then she had felt, somehow, more at her ease than for months and months before; she didn't know why, but her time at the Museum, oddly, had done it." [4] The contrast to Milly Theale, who finds an entirely different refuge in the arts, is immediately apparent.

Dresses, museums, collections, and her own princely room where she can sit "as if she had been carried there prepared, all attired and decorated, like some holy image in a procession," [5] all provide an escape from the cares and pains of life. But the "cracked" situation in her family is a pain she cannot avoid. She would like best to go through life "with bandaged eyes," [6] but she can always find another way of hiding, and her images of pictures and medallions, porcelains, and pagodas, give her imaginatively the arts with which to insulate her sensibilities. She finds it easy to create her own little refuge, and ironically she continually shows, as James says of her, "something of the glitter of consciously possessing the constructive, the creative hand." [7] It is fitting that so many of the images by which she thinks of her situation should be drawn from architecture, for she must deliberately construct them, block by block, for herself.

Maggie, not completely without self-knowledge, does toward the end of the novel catch a faint glimmer of the meaning of the arts for herself. Searching for a birthday present for her father, she has an obscure feeling that an ugly object comes nearer to expressing true human feelings than a beautiful one: "The infirmity of art was the candour of affection, the grossness of pedigree the refinement of sympathy; the ugliest objects, in fact, as a general thing, were the bravest, the tenderest mementos, and, as such, figured in glass cases apart, worthy doubtless of the home, but not worthy of the temple—dedicated to the grimacing, not the clear-faced, gods." [8] Art and the truth are opposites for Maggie, and this opposition gives an added thematic value to the golden bowl. For with its discovery she discovers the truth, and the truth colors the appearance of the bowl: "The golden bowl put on, under consideration, a sturdy, a conscious perversity; as a 'document,' somehow, it was ugly, though it might have a decorative grace." [9] With the breaking of the bowl, making it truly ugly, Maggie feels the decision before her, to continue her old easy way of life or to try another and a more painful: "It was a scene she might people, by the press of her spring, either with serenities and dignities and decencies, or with terrors and shames and ruins, things as

4. Ibid., *2*, 161–2.
5. Ibid., *2*, 158.
6. Ibid., *2*, 189.
7. Ibid., *2*, 151.
8. Ibid., *2*, 162–3.
9. Ibid., *2*, 172.

ugly as those formless fragments of her golden bowl." [1] Retreat or attack, beauty or ugliness, are offered as clear alternatives.

The shattered bowl, with all the symbolic suggestiveness of the shattering, retains its value, in its very ugliness, as a symbol of the truth for Maggie. She says to the Prince, " 'Its having come apart makes an unfortunate difference for its beauty, its artistic value, but none for anything else. Its other value is just the same—I mean that of its having given me so much of the truth about you.' " [2] As an object of beauty it had represented the perfect happiness which Maggie had so desired:

> "I want a happiness without a hole in it big enough for you to poke in your finger."
> "A brilliant, perfect surface—to begin with at least. I see."
> "The golden bowl—as it *was* to have been." And Maggie dwelt musingly on this obscured figure.[3]

But from the beginning the bowl had a crack, and in the complex symbolism of the novel that crack suggested not only the false situation of the relations among the persons of the novel, but also Maggie's false attitude toward the situation, her desire to ignore the truth of evil and to hide within her mental refuge: "The breakage stood not for any wrought discomposure among the triumphant three—it stood merely for the dire deformity of her attitude toward them." [4] The golden bowl, Maggie's imagery of the arts, and her personal relationship with the arts, all inextricably mingled, help to make clear the moral judgment which must be exercised upon her, a judgment which James characteristically leaves to the reader.

Just as Maggie thinks of the good of others while protecting her own comfort, the Prince and Charlotte think of the good of others while enjoying their adulterous affair. The Prince protests at the end of the novel, " 'If ever a man, since the beginning of time, acted in good faith—!' " [5] He can, within his confused conscience, say it in all honesty, for both he and Charlotte have tried not simply to hide the affair from the others, but also to protect and please them. Even Charlotte feels a responsibility toward her husband: " 'I've got so much, by my marriage . . . that I should deserve no charity if I stinted my return. Not to do that, to give back on the contrary all one can, are just one's decency and one's honour and one's virtue. These things, henceforth, . . . are my rule of life, the absolute little gods of my worship, the holy images set up on the wall.' " [6] Within this twisted moral code, curiously unhypo-

1. Ibid., *2*, 242.
2. Ibid., *2*, 196.
3. Ibid., *2*, 222.
4. Ibid., *2*, 246–7.
5. Ibid., *2*, 358.
6. Ibid., *1*, 323.

THE FINAL SYNTHESIS

critical in effect, they pursue their pleasures and satisfy their consciences. As Mrs. Assingham says, expressing the central paradox of the theme, " 'They're really so embroiled but because, in their way, they've been so improbably *good.*' " [7]

Somewhat like Maggie too, the Prince and Charlotte use the arts as a means of self-protection. Most obviously, they use them to hide their guilty secret. When Charlotte, visiting the Prince alone, wants the others to think she is spending the day innocently, she first visits the National Gallery. Later the two take a day alone together in the country, relying for protection on the common knowledge of their love of cathedrals. Yet for the Prince at least, if not for Charlotte, the cathedral town of Gloucester, "with its great church and its high accessibility, its towers that distinguishably signalled, its English history, its appealing type, its acknowledged interest," has a particular meaning, a meaning inherent in its first appearance as a "brave darker wash of far-away watercolour." [8] It seems to represent a symbol of a personal freedom "as perfect and rounded and lustrous as some huge precious pearl." [9] For the Prince, thinking himself an honest man, finds in the arts a personal symbol of the division between public and private life, the wall of decency which he maintains about his own affairs.

The Prince finds personal meaning in the arts, but makes no conscious use of them. Charlotte, on the other hand, uses them deliberately to disguise her feelings and her actions, just as she is forced to lead all of her life. When she wants to sound Maggie's knowledge, yet hide her own actions, she draws Maggie away from the quiet smoking room of Mr. Verver's magnificent country house to the windows of the pompous drawing room with its gilts and glitters, its portraits and lusters. The room has an artificial atmosphere in which Charlotte feels her artificial position will best bear scrutiny: "Here Charlotte again paused, and it was again as if she were pointing out what Maggie had observed for herself, the very look the place had of being vivid in its stillness, of having, with all its great objects as ordered and balanced as for a formal reception, been appointed for some high transaction, some real affair of state." [1] Even when Charlotte wants to be alone to think out her situation she instinctively turns to the ornate summerhouse, "a sort of umbrageous temple, an ancient rotunda, pillared and statued, niched and roofed." [2]

To the very end of the story Charlotte manages to maintain her careful poise, the pride of the secrecy and disguise which Maggie knowingly allows her to retain, and the fact is expressed in characteristic imagery:

7. Ibid., *1*, 403.
8. Ibid., *1*, 365.
9. Ibid., *1*, 366.
1. Ibid., *2*, 252.
2. Ibid., *2*, 318.

"The shade of the official, in her beauty and security, never for a moment dropped; it was a cool, high refuge, like the deep, arched recess of some coloured and gilded image, in which she sat and smiled and waited." [3] She and the Prince maintain a pretence before the eyes of the world, almost without knowing it, and one of the ironies of the novel is the similar imagery by which they and Maggie, all three, picture the situation: "They learned fairly to live in the perfunctory; they remained in it as many hours of the day as might be; it took on finally the likeness of some spacious central chamber in a haunted house, a great overarched and overglazed rotunda, where gaiety might reign, but the doors of which opened into sinister circular passages." [4] The suggestion of deliberation and massive construction gives point to their story, and emphasizes, in its very indirection, the sensitive moral theme of the novel.

Charlotte and the Prince, Maggie and her father, are all avoiding, in their own way, the direct confrontation of the truth. Mr. Verver substitutes esthetic appreciation for normal human relationship; the Prince finds his excuse for misbehavior in a moral dichotomy suggested by the arts; Charlotte uses the arts as one means of hiding her true emotions; Maggie erects a barrier of the arts between the truth and her mental comfort. Stephen Spender in his comments on *The Golden Bowl* says, "The struggle of the Ververs is a struggle to make the picture fit the frame; they are constantly struggling to make their lives worthy of their dead surroundings." [5] In a sense he is right, but he would be more suggestive if he said the Ververs are constantly struggling to substitute their dead surroundings for their lives. The Prince and Charlotte try to live only by carefully formulated rules of generous conduct, and when overcome by more instinctive emotions try to hide the fact from others. But Maggie and her father, more successful in their attempt, defeat any natural emotions by erecting about them a series of rational defenses against the truth which might destroy their artificial inner world. It is over these defenses, defined by the arts, that the moral battle rages.

With characteristic ambiguity, James never makes clear whether Maggie, who represents the principal interest of the novel, finally succumbs to the truth or whether she continues to guard her little comfort. At the end of the novel, in answer to the Prince's question of whether he should have showed more handsomely his acceptance of her knowledge, she says, " 'It isn't a question of any beauty, . . . it's only a question of the quantity of truth.' " [6] This is the lesson of the golden bowl, and Maggie's reunion with her husband, together with her separation from her father, might seem to indicate how well she has learned the les-

---

3. Ibid., *2*, 365.
4. Ibid., *2*, 297.
5. Stephen Spender, *The Destructive Element* (Boston and New York, Houghton Mifflin Co., 1936), p. 91.
6. *Golden Bowl, 2,* 358.

THE FINAL SYNTHESIS   113

son. But the final parting from her father suggests the same old moral blindness. They are admiring a favorite picture which he is leaving behind, almost as a part of himself:

> "It's all right, eh?"
> "Oh, my dear—rather!"
> He had applied the question to the great fact of the picture, as she had spoken for the picture in reply, but it was as if their words for an instant afterwards symbolised another truth, so that they looked about at everything else to give them this extension.[7]

The other objects of art in the room seem to speak to them in the same obscure manner, and in answer to his final comment, " 'Le compte y est. You've got some good things,' " she says, " 'Ah, don't they look well?' "[8] One wonders whether Maggie is not again drifting into her private world of the arts where all is peace and comfort, and the ugly facts of life are forcibly excluded.

The moral decision, then, is never decisively made, even in the separation of the family, and Maggie's form of protected innocence, her own means of escape from what she calls "the great trap of life,"[9] may continue on beyond its first great trial. Fanny Asingham and her practical husband, in their chorus-like role, have already pointed to the tragic aspect of her story:

> "The state of things existing hasn't grown, like a field of mushrooms, in a night. Whatever they, all round, may be in for now is at least the consequence of what they've *done*. Are they mere helpless victims of fate?"
> Well, Fanny at last had the courage of it. "Yes—they are. To be so abjectly innocent—that *is* to be victims of fate."[1]

The innocence of the Ververs, the flaw which makes them victims, is in the last analysis a moral weakness, a lack of will to fight with all their strength against that very fate. The visual arts, which might have signified for them, as for Milly Theale or Isabel Archer, all the accumulated strength of humankind, they have used as a refuge of moral weakness.

With the moral sense so much a part of the esthetic sense, and with both so firmly imbedded in the problem of the American in Europe, Henry James has brought his central themes to a triumphant common conclusion in *The Golden Bowl* as in *The Ambassadors* and, perhaps most successfully, in *The Wings of the Dove*. As the reader looks back over all the novels as well as over James' own relations with the visual arts, the thematic patterns of both fall into a development and a unity

7. Ibid., *2*, 368.
8. Ibid., *2*, 369.
9. Ibid., *2*, 234.
1. Ibid., *1*, 401.

which is impressive for its consistency as well as for its natural integrity. One is tempted to say with James himself, as he thinks of the prefaces to his novels, "These notes represent, over a considerable course, the continuity of an artist's endeavour, the growth of his whole operative consciousness." [2] Neither his esthetic history nor his development of themes nor his presentation of those themes by means of the arts does represent his whole operative consciousness, of course, but in sum they do point the way toward a greater understanding of it, just as the arts point the way toward greater understanding of his novels themselves. Together they incorporate one large segment of his mind, and illustrate one element of his art of the novel; and in a mind and an art so organically unified, one element goes far toward representing the whole.

In retrospect, the themes of the novels, dramatized and defined by the visual arts, and James' own view of the arts meet most conclusively in James' critical conviction that the arts find much of their value and their essence in the power of suggestion and evocation. If the "intellectual charm" of great art lies in its power to suggest a view of human life, a series of relationships with the world about it, even the essence of its own times, it is altogether fitting that it should have this same power in a novel, another form of art which itself plays the same role. And so in those earlier novels in which James shows a particular interest in a definition of the international contrast between America and Europe, the visual arts by their natural power of representation lead the reader into the heart of the definition. Europe is the land of the arts, and its historical and social consciousness is that of its arts. America is the land without art, and its lack of a sensitive historical or social consciousness is reflected in it lack of the arts. This is the international situation which James found for himself, and conditioned as his mind was by his own view of the arts, he turned to what must have seemed a natural means of expressing that view. One is reminded of the passage in *A Small Boy and Others* in which James writes of early visits to the Louvre: "I had looked at pictures, looked and looked again, . . . but I had also looked at France and looked at Europe, looked even at America as Europe itself might be conceived so to look, looked at history, as a still-felt past and a complacently personal future, at society, manners, types, characters, possibilities and prodigies and mysteries of fifty sorts." [3]

As James' interest shifted to a more exclusive—or perhaps more inclusive—moral examination of the individual, moral in terms of a sensitivity to the rigors and the possibilities of the human lot, he once again turned to the visual arts for definition and for dramatization. If the value of art lies in its relationship to human life, one means of defining the

---

2. Preface to *Roderick Hudson,* Collected Novels and Tales (New York, Charles Scribner's Sons, 1907), *I*, vi.
3. *Small Boy,* pp. 351–2.

moral position of an individual is to show his particular view of the arts: is he sensitive to the human values suggested there, and so indirectly to life itself, or does he ignore with a sort of moral blindness the true values in favor of a sterile estheticism? Mere love of art is no test; the test is in the values for which the art is loved. Of course if there is no affection for art at all, the test cannot be applied, but the lack of appreciation is itself a form of blindness which has derogatory implications of the moral state of the individual. Within the numerous dramatic possibilities presented by this means of moral identification, James wrote those novels of his middle life, called here the second group, which carried him to the period of experimentation leading to the final synthesis of the two themes in his last three full novels. These final novels themselves, *The Wings of the Dove, The Ambassadors,* and *The Golden Bowl,* provide the natural summary of James' development and presentation of theme, and by implication the development of his own esthetic consciousness. In them the constant awareness of the evocative and suggestive qualities of art reaches a point of summary, and Milly Theale, surrounded by the arts of Venice, can stand as a moving symbol of the meaning and the value of the arts to Henry James and to his novels.

Index of References to James' Works

Ambassadors, 78, 97–102, 113, 115
American, 23–4, 28–39, 44–6, 48, 80–1, 89
"American Art-Scholar: Charles Eliot Norton," 13–14
American Scene, 8, 11–12, 16, 40, 47
"Art of Fiction," 21–2
"Author of Beltraffio," 59
Awkward Age, 78–9, 82–4

"Beldonald Holbein," 64
"Bethnal Green Museum," 15, 20
"Boston," 16, 19
Bostonians, 23, 40, 44–7

Confidence, 23, 37–8, 40
"Contemporary Notes on Whistler vs. Ruskin," 13

"Dutch and Flemish Pictures in New York," 16

English Hours, 8
Europeans, 23–4, 40, 44, 47–52, 80
["Exhibition in Boston"], 19

Golden Bowl, 24, 61, 78, 81, 97, 102–13, 115
"Grosvenor Gallery and Royal Academy," 15–16, 18

Hawthorne, 12

Italian Hours, 8
Ivory Tower, 23, 40–1

Letters of Henry James, xi, 3–4, 9, 24, 53, 78–9, 98
"Liar," 70
Little Tour in France, 8, 11
"London Exhibitions—Royal Academy," 20

"London Pictures and London Plays," 20

Middle Years, 1, 8

Notebooks, 79, 85, 100–1
Notes of a Son and Brother, 1–3

"On Some Pictures Lately Exhibited," 13, 15, 17, 20
Other House, 78–80, 82, 88
Outcry, 78–82, 103

Picture and Text, 5, 13–17, 19, 21
"Picture Season in London," 15–16, 18–19
["Portrait by Copley"], 16
Portrait of a Lady, 23–4, 37, 39, 53–66, 72, 75, 77, 80, 95, 104, 113
Portraits of Places, 8, 10, 12, 14
Princess Casamassima, 23, 53, 66–9, 72, 89

"Real Thing," 25
Reverberator, 23, 38–40, 53
Roderick Hudson, vii, 23–30, 38, 40, 44, 50, 86, 114

Sacred Fount, 78, 85–8
Sense of the Past, 10, 34, 92, 97
Small Boy and Others, 1, 3, 5–7, 114
Spoils of Poynton, 24, 53–4, 72–7
"Story of a Masterpiece," 70

"Tone of Time," 37, 71
Tragic Muse, 53, 66, 69–72
Transatlantic Sketches, 8–11, 13, 17

Washington Square, 23, 40–4, 48
Watch and Ward, 23, 27–8
What Maisie Knew, 78, 84–5, 88
William Wetmore Story, 8, 10, 12, 19–20
Wings of the Dove, 24, 78, 88–97, 102, 104, 113, 115
"Winter Exhibitions in London," 15